Also by Rich Cohen

THE ADVENTURES OF
HERBIE COHEN

THE ADVENTURES OF
HERBIE COHEN
WORLD'S GREATEST
NEGOTIATOR

BY HIS YOUNGEST SON,

RICH COHEN

FARRAR, STRAUS AND GIROUX
NEW YORK

Farrar, Straus and Giroux
120 Broadway, New York 10271

Printed in the United States of America
First edition, 2022

Library of Congress Cataloging-in-Publication Data
Names: Cohen, Rich, author.
Title: The adventures of Herbie Cohen : world's greatest
 negotiator / by his youngest son, Rich Cohen.
Description: First edition. | New York : Farrar, Straus and
 Giroux, 2022.
Identifiers: LCCN 2021059703 | ISBN 9780374169619
 (hardcover)
Subjects: LCSH: Cohen, Herb. | Cohen, Rich—Family. |
 Jews—New York (State)—New York—Biography. |
 Fathers and sons—United States—Biography. |
 Consultants—United States—Biography. | Negotiation—
 United States—History. | Bensonhurst (New York,
 N.Y.)—Biography.
Classification: LCC F129.B7 C73 2022 | DDC 929.20973—
 dc23/eng/20220126
LC record available at https://lccn.loc.gov/2021059703

Designed by Janet Evans-Scanlon

Our books may be purchased in bulk for promotional,
educational, or business use. Please contact your local
bookseller or the Macmillan Corporate and Premium
Sales Department at 1-800-221-7945, extension 5442,
or by email at MacmillanSpecialMarkets@macmillan.com.

www.fsgbooks.com
www.twitter.com/fsgbooks • www.facebook.com/fsgbooks

10 9 8 7 6 5 4 3 2 1

For Ellen Cohen, who never could stand Larry

When I die, your mother will meet a man who will buy her gifts and flowers, who will do all the little things I was never good at, and who will ask your mother to marry. I tell you now so you know: this man is a schmuck.

—HERB COHEN IN CONVERSATION

THE ADVENTURES OF
HERBIE COHEN

No. 1

MY FATHER DID A LOT OF INSTRUCTING, BUT WE DID NOT always take away the lesson he intended. He taught us in both ways: by example and by counterexample. The most helpful instruction might come via a side remark or gesture, the slouch of his shoulders or a smile that started in his eyes and spread across his face. If a certain song, Frank Sinatra's "There Used to Be a Ballpark," say, struck him as profound, he'd say, "Listen to the words! It's not about a ballpark! It's about life!" If a movie made him cry, Frank Capra's *Mr. Deeds Goes to Town*, for example, he'd say, "It's not about a hayseed from Mandrake Falls. It's about everyone."

Or maybe he did know; maybe he meant for us to learn less from the words than from the music. Maybe it was all misdirection. He could be tricky that way. It's what he meant by the difference between the *what* and the *how*.

"*What* you say is often less important than *how* you say it," he'd explain. "It's like the difference between the head and the heart, between the knowing and the believing."

Consider the way he taught my sister, my brother, and me how to drive. After drilling us on every road sign, traffic custom, and law, and coaching us through every sort of K-turn, lane change, and merge, he'd announce the lesson over, pick a seemingly random destination—Michael's, in Highland Park, for hot dogs, say, or Walker Bros. The Original Pancake House in Wilmette—and tell us to "take it easy and drive me there." Then, as you made the turn in to traffic, he'd slug you hard in the ribs, steady the wheel if you swerved, and say, "You just failed the test: what to do if stung by a bee."

At the end of our last lesson, he told me to drive him to Wrigley Field, where the Chicago Cubs were playing the New York Mets at 3:05 p.m. There was a long line for the left-turn lane that led to the expressway. When we got near the front, my father, who'd been smoking a cigar and tuning the radio, said, "The car in front of you is going to jump the green light and take the left before the oncoming traffic. I want you to get close on his bumper and follow him through."

Explaining himself, he added, "We don't want to miss the first inning."

I started well, and kept close to the lead car, but then made the mistake of looking into the faces of the oncoming drivers. Their eyes were full of hate, their mouths twisted in fury. I froze in the middle of the intersection, snarling traffic and setting off a cacophony of honks and insults. When the cars were finally sorted, we drove on in silence. It was my father who spoke first, saying, "It was my fault. I overestimated you."

When I turned twenty-one, Herbie—of course, to me he's Dad—took me to buy a car. It was to be my first negotiation, an experience akin in his mind to losing one's virginity. He made a long list in preparation for this transaction, a catalog of features my first car had to have. Each characteristic of each candidate was given a number value between one and twenty-two. According to this list, the perfect vehicle for me was a used Honda Civic with less than seventy thousand miles.

We looked and looked; then, amazingly, he balked when we actually found it.

"I don't get you," I said hotly. "It checks every one of your boxes."

"You haven't learned a thing," he said sadly. "This car has all the *what*, but it's seriously deficient in the *how*."

"What are you talking about?"

"Did you see all that writing?"

The car was covered with names. Red letters on the driver's door said "Bobby." Blue letters on the passenger's door said "Bari." Yellow letters on the hood said "Billy," this presumably being the name of the car itself.

"So what?" I said. "We can have it repainted."

"You're missing the point," he told me. "A schmuck owned this car."

No. 2

MY FATHER IS NAMED HERBERT COHEN, BUT MOST PEOPLE call him Herbie. To Grandma Esther he was Herbela. To childhood friends, he is, at his own insistence, Handsomo, Mr. Stunning, or the Elder Statesman. In professional circles, he is Herb Cohen, an expert in the art of the deal and the author of *You Can Negotiate Anything*, a publishing phenomenon that came out of nowhere in 1980 to sell more than a million copies. He's a speaker, a guru of the corporate retreat, a consultant to governments and companies, the gun hired to work out the terms and close the deal, the wise man helicoptered in to settle the strike. He helped resolve the Major League Baseball umpires' strike in 1979, as well as the New Orleans Police strike the same year. He advised Jimmy Carter during the Iran hostage crisis in 1980 and 1981. He advised Ronald Reagan during the summits with Mikhail Gorbachev in 1985 and 1986. He was part of the American team at

Geneva during the Strategic Arms Reduction Talks in the 1980s, where he went "eyeball to eyeball with the Russkies" and learned what he calls "the Soviet style." He helped settle the NFL players' strike in 1987.

He trained G-men and spooks. He was a pioneer in the field of game theory and helped set up the FBI's Behavioral Science Unit. The famous term he might well have coined— "win-win"—comes from game theory, which, according to Herbie, focused on potential outcomes, including "win-lose," "lose-win," "lose-lose," and "win-win," which he merely re-purposed from academic study to human relations. And yet, though he's lectured at Harvard and Yale and worked for many Fortune 500 companies, including IBM, Apple, Google, General Motors, Sony, and Samsung, he says he learned everything he needed to know about negotiation in Brooklyn as a kid, citing a specific incident. "A tenth grader snatched a dog off the street and took it into a basement. He said he'd kill the dog if its owner, a girl who went to Erasmus—she was my friend Inky's cousin—did not go to a dance with him. A classic kidnapping. I was the only one on the scene who could figure out how to talk to the kid, understand and reason with him. As for learning the trade, it had everything: a victim, a hysterical family, an unreasonable demand, a crowd of on-lookers, and a ticking clock. We all had to be home in time for dinner."

By 5:30 p.m., Herbie having persuaded the kidnapper to settle for a free lunch at a diner of his choice instead of a date, the dog was safely back home and the street returned to its former placidity.

Over time, Herbie turned the tricks he learned in coastal

Brooklyn—he's from Bensonhurst, looks like it, and talks like it—into a philosophy, a kind of Jewish Buddhism. He preaches engaged detachment, characterized as "caring, but not that much." More than a business strategy, he considers this a way of life. "Don't get fixated on a particular outcome," he says. "Always be willing to walk away—from the car, from the house, from the property. Once you see your life as a game, and the things you strive for as no more than pieces in that game, you'll become a much more effective player."

Most of his parental advice is about maintaining perspective, which he does by dismissing whatever is currently bothering you as "a walnut in the batter of life, a blip on the radar screen of eternity." The man is besotted with aphorisms. If you look and look at something, but still can't see what he wants you to see, he'll say, "We're all captives of the pictures in our heads." Or: "We see things not as they are but as we are." Or: "Believing is seeing." If you present him with a clever plan to right a previous wrong, he'll say, "The meek shall inherit the earth, but not its mineral rights." If you are mesmerized by a charismatic leader, he'll say, "The key to walking on water is knowing where the stones are." Or: "Don't put your trust in princes."

"Time heals all wounds," he'd once told me, "right up to the moment it kills you."

No. 3

HERBIE GREW UP IN THE REDBRICK APARTMENT HOUSE AT 2109 Eighty-Fifth Street in Bensonhurst, Brooklyn, near the intersection with Twenty-First Avenue. If you go today, you'll find Ichi Sushi, Amazing Aquarium, BeBe Day Spa, Lily Bloom Bakery, Gap, and Effie's Boutique.

Bensonhurst is grittier than the more famous neighborhoods to the north—Park Slope, Carroll Gardens, Red Hook, Cobble Hill, Dumbo. Untouched by gentrification, it's Brooklyn as it used to be, fog shrouded, provincial, and cozy, and the traffic sounds like surf, and the church bells sound like buoys. It's still mostly mom-and-pop stores in Bensonhurst, pizzerias and taverns, a neon martini glass in the window, auto-body repair, smoke shops, kids at work on their bodies and machines. The record man Seymour Stein once told me that "only two notable people ever came out of Bensonhurst: Vic Damone and Seymour Stein." Herbie keeps a longer list. "How about Sandy Koufax?" he says. "How about Elliott Gould, John Franco, Carl Sagan? How about Sammy 'the Bull' Gravano?"

To Herbie, Bensonhurst was home, and Manhattan was the city. Distant, romantic, unattainable. Talking about a neighborhood character who never got out, one of my father's old friends will say, "He hasn't even been to the *city* in forty years!" Herbie sometimes describes the Bensonhurst of his youth as "a shtetl on Gravesend Bay." Asked to account for the large Italian population, he adds, "It was Calabria, too." Here's how he breaks down the overall demographics: "48 percent Jewish, 50 percent Italian, 2 percent Other."

Herbie's childhood apartment was ideally situated—a block and a half from the center of the known world, the busy intersection where the fathers ascended the stairs of the elevated in the morning and descended them in the evening, where candy shops, cigar stores, and newsstands crowded into an urban quintessence and the streetlamps burned all night.

A Brooklyn kid in that era was less affiliated with a family or a school than with a corner, a headquarters where he could bullshit for hours. Herbie and his friends were based out of Eighty-Fifth and Bay Parkway the way the 101st Airborne is based out of Fort Campbell, Kentucky. It's where they planned and prepared, and where they always returned. They were at home at Eighty-Fifth and Bay Parkway the way Thomas Jefferson was at home in Monticello, Hugh Hefner was at home in the Playboy Mansion, John Gotti was at home at the Ravenite Social Club on Mulberry Street in Little Italy. It's where they tested the identities they'd assume in the world; it's where they became themselves.

Brooklyn was nothing but corners in the 1950s and 1960s—some friendly, some neutral, some to be avoided. A kid dumped into an unfamiliar neighborhood by a broken subway made his way back to Eighty-Fifth Street and Bay Parkway in the manner of Odysseus island-hopping to Ithaca, progressing from adventure to misadventure until he spotted the familiar light of Lenny's Pizza.

I don't know what Herbie's apartment looked like inside. All the pictures are close-ups. You might see a vase or a couch in the background, but no more. Which doesn't bother Herbie. You'll never meet a less nostalgic person. When he talks about the past, it's not rooms or cities or songs he describes; it's nicknames, jokes, faces. Once, when I returned from a vacation with pictures of beautiful landscapes, he scolded me, saying, "Where are the people? The faces? In ten years, it's not that geyser you'll want to see. It's the faces of your friends."

Herbie was eight when the Japanese attacked Pearl Harbor. He followed the war in the newspapers and newsreels, but got a better sense of the stakes by eavesdropping on his father's brothers, who gathered once a week to discuss business—the business of their business and the business of the war. These men, who worked together in the garment trade—Grandpa Morris and his siblings owned a small factory that made hat bindings—had emigrated from Poland in the first years of the twentieth century. Tough, humorous men, they spoke a thickly accented mid-century patois of English, Polish, and Yiddish. They'd sit in the living room talking about flanking maneuvers and sea battles. Each uncle had a favorite general—Eisenhower, MacArthur, or Bradley. They might consider a general personally distasteful—"Patton's a real anti-Semite"—yet still appreciate his skill: "But what do I care if he gets the job done?"

Herbie could track the progress of the war in the way his uncles talked about England's commanding general. In the early going, they spoke of him formally as "Field Marshal Bernard Montgomery," saying, "I hope this field marshal Bernard Montgomery knows what he's doing." They dropped the honorific when the tide turned, saying, "Montgomery is a hell of a general!" By the time the Allies were shaking hands with the Soviets on the Elbe River, he was simply "Monty," as in "God Bless Monty!"

Herbie was fighting his own war in the movie theaters of Brooklyn, grand show palaces where gangs of kids staked out territory, erected battlements, and unleashed fusillades of candy. Sneak attacks, suicide missions, glorious last stands—battles waged in the flickering light of the silver screen, where John Wayne and Gregory Peck and Robert Taylor and Jimmy Stewart were going over the top, opening the bomb bay doors, or getting misty-eyed at the thought of democracy. *Sergeant York* was Herbie's favorite. In it, a young pacifist played by Gary Cooper searches for a balance between the holy documents of his life: the Bible, in which God commands, "Thou shalt not kill," and the U.S. Constitution, which must occasionally be defended with force. Asked why he loved that movie, Herbie looks at you as if you were a fool, then says, "Why? Because in it one doughboy captures like five hundred Krauts."

No. 4

THE WORLD WAS DIFFERENT AFTER THE WAR, BUT NO ONE was sure why. There was the breaking news of atrocities, the concentration camps and the ruined cities of Europe, the terror of the bomb, but there was something else, too. As the only Western nation to come through the 1940s intact, America had become a great power by default, and thanks to this emergence the horizon of every American expanded. It was like being a Roman after the Pyrrhic War, or a Brit after the sinking of the Spanish Armada. The change could be felt even if it could not quite be explained. The years that followed were the paradise you recognize only when it's lost. The Depression had ended; the war had been won. American jets patrolled the skies of the world. American soldiers were handsome, wisecracking, clever, and kind. American cities were vibrant and safe. The apartments affordable, the public schools excellent. The kids of that time were living at the top of an arc. It had never been like that before and would never be like that again. It was a bubble that in a moment would pop, but meanwhile the moment expanded into an eternity.

Each afternoon, the students of Bensonhurst P.S. 128 were released like birds from an aviary. Squawking through the streets, they coalesced on the corners to devise another plan and assault another night. Bensonhurst was an ethnic enclave, where a kid believed every adult was a parent who would save him if necessary. Its confines were marked by its architecture of redbrick buildings, concrete storefronts, and that vast outer-borough sky. When you crossed into a new neighborhood, the change was gradual—like moving from hot water to warm water—which warned you and gave you time to chicken out. If you ventured into the unknown, it was only because you really wanted to know. Every kid was Captain Cook in the summer, surveying strange coasts, exploring mysterious islands, trading, or fighting, then sailing home.

The elevated train floated like a ribbon above New Utrecht Avenue, the windows of the cars reflecting traffic lights, telephone poles, clouds. The tracks went belowground in Flatbush, the train becoming a subway as it approached the harbor and metropolis. The IRT was cheap and safe. In Bensonhurst, parents let twelve- and thirteen-year-olds ride with friends to Madison Square Garden or Times Square. A stray dog that lived in a box on Eighty-Sixth Street used to ride the train alone. "He'd get on when we got on, but get off before, usually at Chambers," Herbie told me. "One day, we decided to follow him. We watched him go to the back door of five or six big lunch places and dig scraps out of the trash. Then he went down the stairs and caught the downtown train back to Brooklyn."

Many kids formed into self-governing units, platoons as hierarchical and tradition-bound as those in the military. This was your family outside your family, your corner brothers, your tribe. Though they were known as gangs, their jackets identified them as SACs, social athletic clubs. Mostly they hung around, talking about school and girls, or played sports. Some clubs fielded a basketball, baseball, roller hockey, and football team. SACs tended to cohere by ethnicity. There were Black gangs, Asian gangs, Irish gangs, Italian gangs, and Jewish gangs, each associated with a particular corner. My father was a member of the Warriors, a gang that rendezvoused at Eighty-Sixth Street and Bay Parkway.

The name was opportunistic as well as fierce. There was a Pontiac dealer in Bensonhurst, and as anyone could tell you, Pontiac's logo was an Indian head. By swiping signs from the lot, the boys furnished their bedrooms and interior spaces with professional-grade insignia. To the members of other local gangs—the Screaming Wizards, the Coney Island Canaries—the name seemed either aspirational or ironic. Though most of the Warriors would defend themselves in a pinch, few of them were battlers. My father, as a leader of the gang, can stand for the typical Warrior: even then, he was less Achilles than Odysseus, a wily man, a clever navigator who'd rather think than slug his way across the archipelago.

I was raised on stories about the Warriors. The names of the members are a lyric in my imagination, summoning stoops and basement rooms, meetings in lamplight and confessions in candlelight, air shafts and alleys, clotheslines hung with Hawaiian shirts, polyester slacks, and candy-colored socks, images from a childhood more varied and interesting than my own.

Inky, Sheppo, Bucko, Who Ha, Ben the Worrier, Iron Lung, Gutter Rat, who was called that even by his own

mother—"Hey, Gutter Rat, time for dinner!"—Zeke the Creek the Mouthpiece. Inky because he drank a bottle of ink on a dare. Sheppo because he looked like a lost Marx brother. Bucko because his real name was Buckholtz. Who Ha because, one night, when asked a question, he said, "Who?" then, when that question was repeated, he said, "Huh?" *His* real name was Bernie Horowitz. Ben the Worrier because of his crippling neurosis. Iron Lung because he could swim five lengths at the community pool on a single breath. Gutter Rat because he looked like a gutter rat. Zeke the Creek the Mouthpiece because Zeke was short for Zeiger, because Creek rhymed with Zeke, because he announced events on the corner like a paid radio mouthpiece.

Herbie first met Larry Zeiger at school when they were no more than nine years old. As potential incorrigibles, the boys had been deputized by the administration—this is called co-opting—fitted with orange sashes, and sent to work as crossing guards on the corner of Seventy-Sixth Street and Nineteenth Avenue, near the side entrance of school. Larry, whose father had recently died of a heart attack—he'd owned a bar in Bay Ridge—searched for a replacement in everyone he loved, starting with fourth-grade Herbie, who was more than happy to advise, guide, and lead Larry into and out of trouble. They started debating in the street, arguing. Larry said that crossing kids on their way to school was busywork, a joke.

Herbie disagreed.

"It's a position with real power," he said.

After a few nickels were wagered, Herbie walked to the middle of Nineteenth Avenue and held up his hand, bringing traffic to a stop.

"It's as simple as this," Herbie said over his shoulder.

He was proving what would become a lifelong principle: most people are schmucks and will obey any type of authority, even if it's just a nine-year-old in an orange sash. (As he'd say later in lectures, "Power is based on perception; if you think you got it, you got it, even if you don't got it.") Cars and trucks were soon backed up for blocks. There was honking and cursing. Several people got out of their vehicles. A teacher came to investigate. Larry and Herbie were sent to the principal, who tore off their sashes with ceremony. A lifelong friendship had been born.

No. 5

TAKING A NICKNAME WAS AN ACT OF RITUAL IMPORTANCE in the neighborhood, akin to a bar mitzvah or christening. It was a step away from home, a step into your life in the pack. As I said, my father was called Handsomo. He stares with confusion when asked how he got that name, then says, "I'm a good-looking man."

"He *was* good-looking compared to the other Warriors," Larry (a.k.a. Zeke) told me. "He had black hair and green eyes, a very unusual combination on Eighty-Sixth Street and Bay Parkway. And look at some of the old clubhouse pictures. We were a homely group."

When I asked my grandma Esther—my father's mother—the same question, she said, "Handsomo? I know that's what he asked the boys to call him."

The Warriors wore maroon jackets with white letters. The jackets were reversible, worn inside out—white with maroon letters—to dances, weddings, going-away parties, and graduations. These jackets hung from hooks by the door of the clubroom on Seventy-Ninth Street in Bensonhurst, the basement of Bernie Horowitz's house. Who Ha lived upstairs with his mother, father, sister, and grandmother, known to everyone as Bubba. A glow-in-the-dark Indian was painted on the wall of the clubroom. The light was dim, the radio tuned to Sinatra, but what the old Warriors really remember is the sound of Bubba, who, per doctor's orders, was rolled across the floor upstairs twice a day to improve her circulation.

The clubhouse had been furnished slowly, piece by piece, via thievery.

Larry: "Bucko's father was a mechanic."

Herbie: "He had extra coveralls."

Larry: "We'd each put on a pair, then go from apartment house to apartment house."

Herbie: "When the doorman came out, we'd tell him . . ."

Larry: "Or super. Sometimes, it was a super."

Herbie: ". . . that we'd been hired to take the couch for reupholstering."

Larry: "Sometimes the super would hold the door for us."

Herbie: "I'd slip the guy a dollar on the way out and say, 'Thank you.'"

No. 6

THE GLORY OF CARTHAGE SURVIVES IN A SINGLE STORY. That's how history works. It's not what happened, but what remains when everything else has been forgotten. The Warriors survive in two stories, which Zeke the Creek, who later changed his name to Larry King, told, elaborated, and retold on the radio until they'd become legends. In 1994, one of these stories was written up by Alec Wilkinson and published in *The New Yorker* as "The Mouthpiece and Handsomo." But to us, it's always been "The Moppo Story."

It starts with Herbie, Larry, and their friend Brazie Abbate, who later became a brain surgeon, picking up Gil Mermelstein—Moppo, because of his unruly hair—for the first day of eighth grade. Moppo's house was dark; a cousin was waiting on the stoop. He said Moppo, who'd always been sickly, had been diagnosed with tuberculosis and had gone with his parents to Arizona for the treatment. "As soon as I'm finished closing the house," the cousin said, "I'm going in to tell the school."

This is where the story forks, where, though it could have gone this way, it went that way instead.

"Let us help," Herbie told Moppo's cousin.

"How?"

"We'll tell the school what happened. We're going there, anyway."

"Really? That'd be great. Thank you."

Herbie, Larry, and Brazie walked on in silence.

In Larry's version, Herbie then says, "I've got a good idea for how to make a little money."

Larry: "Yeah? What?"

Herbie: "We go to the front office; then, instead of telling them Moppo went to Arizona, we tell them Moppo died. Then we go around and raise money for a funeral wreath."

Larry: "That's crazy."

Brazie: "What happens when Moppo comes back?"

Herbie: "When will that be? Next fall? We'll be in high school. Dr. Armor"—Dr. Gene Armor was the principal of P.S. 128—"won't be able to do anything."

And so they went to the front office and told the staff that Gil Mermelstein was dead, then told their teachers and classmates, then went from room to room raising money, then went to Coney Island and spent the money on hot dogs and rides.

From the top of the Wonder Wheel, you can see every roof in Brooklyn.

Herbie's version is more innocent. He says that it all

started when a kid asked him why Moppo wasn't at school. Herbie told him about the tuberculosis, but the kid didn't believe him, told him to stop joking, and asked again, "Where's Moppo?" Herbie told him a second time—tuberculosis, Arizona. Anyone who knows Herbie also knows he has a rule. If you ask him a question, he will tell you the truth. If you ask again, you will again get the truth. But if you ask a third time, he will tell you whatever he thinks you want to hear. So, when the kid asked what happened to Moppo a third time, Herbie said, "Moppo is dead."

"A few hours later, the story was everywhere," Herbie says. "That's really how it began. I didn't have some big plan. I just played the hand I'd been dealt. And yes, we went to the office, and yes, we told them Moppo died. The money, the funeral wreath . . . all that's true."

Days turned into weeks. Autumn became winter. By the spring, they'd forgotten all about Moppo in Arizona.

Then came the call from Dr. Armor, the official summons from class.

Herbie, Larry, and Brazie whispered as they waited outside the office.

Brazie: "You said we'd be in high school before anyone found out."

Herbie: "Let's see what he says."

Larry: "He's going to expel us."

Herbie: "No one's getting expelled."

Herbie was right. Dr. Armor did not scold or punish the boys, but praised them—for the kindness they had shown their dead friend, how they'd spoken up for him, raised money for a wreath, and laid that wreath on his grave.

"You're the sort of young men we want in this school," he said, "which is why we've decided to create a new honor, the Gil Mermelstein Memorial Award, which will be given each spring to a student or group of students who have earned the honor through an act of service. You three will be the first winners of the Gil Mermelstein Memorial Award. Tell your parents. There will be an assembly in the auditorium with members of the press invited. The high schools get attention for sports. Here's our chance to shine."

Larry sat on the front steps after school, face in hands, weeping. Brazie had gone from fear to anger. He was furious with Herbie. Who remained calm. "What's changed?" he asked. "Moppo is still in Arizona, and we're still in Bensonhurst, three weeks from graduation. They're giving us an award? Great!"

Larry: "What do we do?"

Herbie: "Nothing. As far as the school's concerned, Moppo is still dead."

The entire student body—more than a thousand kids—gathered in the auditorium for the ceremony. Dr. Armor, in a brown tweed suit with Brylcreemed hair, spoke from the podium. Herbie, Larry, and Brazie sat onstage beneath a banner: "The First Annual Gil Mermelstein Memorial Award." A reporter from *The New York Times* had turned up with a photographer. Meanwhile, having made what Larry calls "the most remarkable recovery in the annals of tubercular medicine," Moppo was walking the halls of P.S. 128, wondering where all the people had gone. A lady in the office sent him to the auditorium.

Larry: "There were two ways into that auditorium, through

a side door inside the school or through the big front doors that led from Eighty-Fourth Street, meaning you had to go outside, walk around, then come back in. That day, for whatever reason, Moppo took the outside doors, which clanged as they slammed shut."

Herbie: "The kids in back turned around to see who'd come late. Most of them recognized Moppo right away and immediately knew what we'd done, and started laughing."

Larry: "The laughter spread through the auditorium, making its way toward the stage. Dr. Armor looks up. But he has no idea who Moppo is and doesn't know what's going on."

Herbie: "Moppo wasn't the smartest person in the world, but he knew what 'memorial' means."

Larry: "It means you're dead."

Herbie: "And he knew you did not want your name next to it."

Larry: "Moppo froze."

Herbie: "No one knew what to do."

Larry: "Herbie jumps to his feet, cups his hands around his mouth, and shouts, 'Go home, Moppo. You're dead!'"

Dr. Armor sent everyone back to class, tore down the banner, smashed the award plaque, then told Herbie, Larry, and Brazie to wait in his office. The *Times* reporter was there, too, asking questions. Dr. Armor sat them in the chairs across from his desk, stared at them for a long, uncomprehending moment, then blew his stack. His voice could be heard all over the building: You'll never go to class again! You'll never play sports again! You'll never graduate from a school again! You'll never get this, you'll never earn that! You'll be expelled, incarcerated, blah, blah, blah.

Herbie raises his hand and says, "Wait a minute, Dr. Armor. You're making a terrible mistake."

"What did you say?" asks Dr. Armor.

Larry told the rest of the story in books, on the radio, on television, and at every variety of Warrior reunion and family function.

"Herbie looks across the desk, calm as can be, and says, 'Slow down, Dr. Armor. Let's talk this through. Yes, we did a very bad thing. We admit it. But if you expel us, there will be a hearing before the Board of Education. That's automatic. At that hearing they'll want to know why you took the word of three idiot kids that another kid was dead, and why, to confirm it, all you did was call the house, get a disconnect message, and mark the kid's card deceased. Yes, we'll be expelled, but you'll be fired. You'll never get another teaching job in New York."

Dr. Armor sat back and groaned. Larry described his demeanor as "totally whipped."

Larry always spoke of this as "Herbie's first negotiation."

"[He] agreed not to suspend us, and we talked to the reporter and said that what we had done was stupid and we were returning the money, and he agreed it was really more of a *Daily News* kind of story," Herbie told *The New Yorker*, "and we went to Moppo's house that afternoon to try to explain what had happened, but to this day I don't think he really understands how we could have said that he was dead."

This experience let Herbie test a theory he'd been working on since his crossing guard days: life is a game, and to win, you must consider other people as players with as much at stake as yourself, if not more. If you understand their motivations, you can control the action and free yourself from every variety of jam. Focus less on yourself and more on others. Everyone has something at stake. If you address that predicament, you can move anyone, even a junior high principal, from no to yes.

Decades later, while Herbie was telling the Moppo story on the radio with Larry, Gil Mermelstein called the station, and a producer put him on the air. Larry welcomed him and had enough time to ask just a few questions before Herbie interrupted, saying, "Go home, Moppo, you're dead," then pressed the disconnect button. That was the last time Herbie and Larry ever spoke to Gil Mermelstein.

No. 7

THE SECOND STORY:

November 1951. Herbie was a seventeen-year-old high school senior with his own car, a Ford Fairlane. He and Larry were arguing on the corner of Eighty-Sixth and Bay Parkway with a kid named Sandy. This was Sandy Koufax, already a neighborhood athletic legend, known not for his pitching but for his passing, rebounding, and shooting; he was the youngest starter on the Jewish Community House's all-star basketball team. People still talk about the night the JCH all-stars hosted the New York Knicks for charity. Koufax did not merely dominate Harry "the Horse" Gallatin, the Knicks' six-foot-six center, but humiliated him.

Sandy was telling Herbie and Larry about a trip his family had taken to New Haven, Connecticut, where they'd been served "three scoops of ice cream for 15 cents" at a Carvel.

"This immediately started a violent argument," Larry wrote in his book *Larry King*, "with Sandy insisting he did get three scoops for 15 cents and Herbie and me arguing that that was impossible."

Within moments, money was in the offing. Herbie bet $5 and Larry bet $3 that a person could purchase three scoops of ice cream for 15 cents in New Haven or anywhere else. Of course, the only way to settle the bet was to drive to New Haven.

They retrieved Herbie's car, then went to Seventy-Ninth Street to pick up Who Ha, because, Larry told us, "you just couldn't make that kind of trip without Bernie."

"Bernie was at dinner with his parents, Dora and Nathan, when we got there," Herbie said. "We asked him to go to Carvel, but did not tell him that the Carvel we had in mind was in New Haven, Connecticut. There must've been fifty Carvels in Brooklyn alone. There was one a block from Bernie's house. Bernie had this weirdly formal way of talking. And he says, 'Mother and Father, here is what I am going to do. I am going to go with Sandy, Larry, and Herbie to Carvel, and since we have eaten dairy, it will be kosher. I will just have some ice cream, then I will come right home.'"

They got in the car and headed north, driving in silence across the borough—all those windows, all those lives. The white tiles of the Brooklyn–Battery Tunnel flashed across the windshield as they crossed into Manhattan. They merged onto the West Side Highway, then followed it past the city, across the Harlem River, and into the Bronx. It was not until Herbie turned onto the Merritt Parkway, where signs pointed to New England, that Who Ha sat up in the backseat and said, "Hey! Where the hell are we going? I told my parents I'd be right home."

He was angry, but forgot his anger when Larry told him about the three scoops.

"Impossible," said Who Ha, who put four of his own dollars into the pot.

New Haven was closing down when they arrived. The streets were empty, the stores dark. It started to snow, at first a few flurries, then flakes, a freak November storm. The lights were still on in the Carvel. A man stood behind the counter, looking out at the snow.

Herbie parked across the street, then sat arguing with his friends.

Larry: "If we just go in there and ask how much for three scoops, he'll know something's doing."

Who Ha: "Yeah. Maybe Sandy set it all up in advance. Maybe this ice cream guy has a piece of the action."

It was decided that Herbie should go in alone, put fifteen cents on the counter, and say, "Give me that much."

Five minutes later, Zeke, Who Ha, and Sandy were sitting in the car, watching Herbie eat three scoops—strawberry, chocolate, vanilla—as he talked with the ice cream man on the other side of the big window.

Herbie raised his cone when his friends came in, saying, "Sandy wins."

After several rounds of ice cream, the counterman asked what it was all about.

"We don't usually get a group of kids having a feast at closing time in the middle of a snowstorm," he explained.

"The guy found it hard to believe that we drove all the way

from Brooklyn just to settle a bet," Larry explained later, "but what he found even more incredible, and the reason, he now realized, that he was going out of business, was that he'd been giving away an extra scoop with each order."

Two inches of snow had fallen by the time the boys were back in the car.

"Let's drive around," said Larry. "I've always wanted to see New Haven."

They went past the Gothic spires of the Yale campus in the snow, past the parks and the monuments, past the football stadium, past the plows lined up on Chapel Street. As they turned onto Butler Street, which would take them back to the Merritt Parkway, they suddenly found themselves in a strange middle-of-the-night traffic jam, cars in front and cars behind, people honking, hanging out windows, waving signs. "I'm following 'em," said Herbie, swinging around to join the parade, which wound through the city and ended at the community center, where everyone parked and went inside.

It was 1:00 a.m. on a Tuesday in November. Election Day. Herbie, Larry, Who Ha, and Sandy had stumbled on a party for volunteers who'd campaigned for Richard Lee, who would serve eight terms as mayor of New Haven before moving to the U.S. Congress.

Sandy stood against a wall in the back as Herbie and Larry worked the crowd. Who Ha was at the buffet table, filling his pockets with donuts.

Pulling Larry aside, Sandy said, "Do you know what Herbie's doing? He's going around, telling all these people that you've been the number one campaigner, that no one's worked as hard as you."

26

Larry, trying to even the score, then went around, talking up Herbie.

The campaign manager stood up and thanked the workers, then shaded his eyes, looked across the crowd, and asked, "Is Zeke out there? All night I've been hearing about the great work this young man Zeke has done for us. Stand up and introduce yourself, Zeke."

Larry stood, waved, then introduced Herbie, saying, "He's the real hero."

"Herbie gets up and starts talking," Larry said later. "He talks for maybe fifteen minutes. He does the history of America, Paul Revere's Night Ride, the Declaration of Independence, and the U.S. Constitution. He whipped the crowd into a frenzy. Then said, 'I give you not just the next Mayor of New Haven, but the next President of the United States: Richard Lee.'"

They got back to Brooklyn at 4:00 a.m., the Ford Fairlane fishtailing through the snowy intersections. There was a foot of snow on the ground. The houses and buildings were dark. In the entire borough, a single light glowed: Who Ha's living room, where Dora and Nathan were peering through the curtains into the street.

Nathan, in robe and slippers, met Herbie's car at the curb. He was red with anger. He lined the boys up on the sidewalk, then, walking before them, poked them one after another in the chest, saying, "Bum. Bum. Bum. You're a bum. You're a bum. You're a bum. Ten years!" He shouted, "Ten years! That's how much of my life you've taken tonight." But when he finally let Who Ha explain where they'd gone and why, he said, "Three scoops for fifteen cents? That's impossible."

Here's what Herbie learned in New Haven: if you say something long enough and loud enough and with enough confidence—"No one has worked harder for this campaign than Zeke"—people will believe you, and once they believe you, you can take as many donuts as you want.

No. 8

HERBIE STARTED COLLEGE AS A COMMUTER STUDENT AT NYU. He did not do well. In fact, he bombed. He wanted a campus like those he'd seen in the Andy Hardy movies, or read about in the Booth Tarkington novels, or glimpsed in New Haven in the snow that night, but his days still started and ended in Bensonhurst. It was the same friends on the corner of Eighty-Sixth Street and Bay Parkway, the same Warriors in the same jackets on the same basketball courts and at the same parties. He tried to give the scene a skip, but the boys would turn up at his apartment, ring the buzzer, then stand on the curb shouting his name. "Yo, Herbie! We're short a player. Do you want us to forfeit?"

Caught in the tide of old friends and habits, he began to skip homework, ditch class, blow off exams. Halfway through freshman year, his report card was a bloodbath of red ink. Meanwhile, he was consumed by fear. Forty thousand Americans were killed in Korea in 1951. Another hundred thousand were wounded, many grievously. It was the worst year of the Korean War. College alone stood between Herbie and the draft. He'd be called up if he failed out, possibly sent to Korea, possibly killed. He could not stop imagining it—his body in every state of defilement and decay, smoke on the fields, the thump of artillery shells, a wave of Chinese soldiers, a mushroom cloud in the distance. In the end, he realized the only way to stop worrying was to get it over with. He quit school and enlisted in the army. He was given two weeks to report. Those last few days were a blur of goodbyes, but he spent his final night alone in his bedroom. The windows were open, a warm breeze blowing. He could see the lights on the avenues, storefronts, cars on the parkway; he could hear ships in the Narrows. This was Brooklyn as it would never be for him again. The past is not what happened but how it felt. He owned a single LP, Frank Sinatra's *Dedicated to You*, which he played again and again as he waited for morning. The songs on that album—"The Moon Was Yellow," "None but the Lonely Heart," "Why Was I Born?"—put him into a blue mood, a melancholy funk. "I listened until dawn," he told me, "then said goodbye to my parents, went to Whitehall Street, and boarded a bus for New Jersey."

No. 9

FORT DIX IS ABOUT TWENTY MILES SOUTH OF TRENTON. Named after an old general, the grounds cover 42,000 acres of pine scrub. To Herbie's eyes, it was exactly like an army base in a movie: perimeter fence, checkpoints, mess hall, barracks, obstacle course, shooting range. First came the physical and mental exams, the haircut, the issuing of uniforms, the induction with right hand raised: "I, Herbert Allan Cohen, do solemnly swear that I will support and defend the Constitution of the United States against all enemies, foreign and domestic; that I will bear true faith and allegiance to the same; and that I will obey the orders of the President of the United States and the orders of the officers appointed over me, according to regulations and the Uniform Code of Military Justice. So help me God."

Families were allowed to visit on weekends. Herbie's parents, uneducated Polish émigrés, took the bus down from Borough Hall. Herbie's division consisted mostly of New Yorkers, many of them Jewish. There was a rabbi at Fort Dix, an old man with a long gray beard who wandered among the relatives, answering questions. Shortly after Herbie's induction, the rabbi addressed the fears of some of the families at a Friday night service. Speaking with a thick Yiddish accent, he said, "I have talked to your commanding officer. A good man, a mensch. I asked where you will complete your training, and he told me and promised me that you boys will be staying right here at Fort Dix. So, tell your mommies and your poppies not to worry, because you will be right here in New Jersey."

The sergeants came through the barracks at three the next morning, banging garbage cans to wake the grunts, who were marched to an airfield, loaded on transport planes, and flown to Camp Chaffee, Arkansas, where their real work began.

Herbie was assigned to a southern division at Camp Chaffee. From then on, he'd be a Yankee among rebels, a Jew among Gentiles, a Brooklyn wiseass among rednecks. "It was only then that I began to understand this country," he told me later.

Camp Chaffee is in the low hills west of Hot Springs. The first weeks there were tougher than anything Herbie had ever experienced. He realized he had hidden reserves in those

weeks, a strength that even he, or especially he, had been un-
aware of. He realized he was better than nobody, but also that
nobody was better than him. He learned how to pack a bag,
make a bed, march in line, sprint in formation. He learned
how to hike, reconnoiter, build a fire, fight with his hands. He
learned how to live out of a sack and keep his gun clean. Now
and then, a sergeant dumped the contents of his foot locker
on the floor, clicked a stopwatch, and timed how long it took
him to get it all repacked. He learned how to shoot a revolver
and assemble a rifle in the dark. He learned how to hit both
kinds of targets—moving and still. He learned how to be a
soldier.

There were classes and tests like at school, but it was okay
to be a little dumb in the army. Maybe it was even preferable.
Very dumb was a problem, but very smart was worse. Maybe
that's where Magna Para went wrong: he was too smart for
his own good. Herbie hated Magna Para at first because
Magna Para made everyone's life difficult, but he'd come to
admire him by the end of basic. Herbie enlisted, but Magna
Para had been drafted against his will and refused to accept
the dominion of officers. He was the man who cannot be
broken.

Judging by accent, Magna Para came from the Ozarks, a
hollow so deep in the hills the sun could hardly penetrate, the
kind of place where an extravagant feast is rabbit and moon-
shine. The origin or meaning of that name—Magna Para—
remained a mystery, another strange aspect of what Herbie
considered the inscrutable South.

Magna Para finished every drill last, lost every race. Even
when running, he seemed to be standing still. Standing at

attention, he seemed to slouch. A short man with ears like pitcher handles, Magna Para radiated ease. He was lectured and threatened, made to stand in the rain, made to do push-ups and sit-ups, run and clean, but nothing seemed to bother Magna Para, ruin his mood, scare him. Always that dopey calm: he was a holy fool, either enlightened or demented, or possibly both.

In the second month of basic training, the sergeant began waking the men in the middle of the night several times a week. Curses, whistles, baseball bats on bed frames. They were told to get up, get dressed, and assemble in formation in the courtyard in less than three minutes. If they failed, they were sent back to do it again. It was the same every time: the men were in line in the yard being inspected when Magna Para appeared at the top of the stairs, shirt untucked, boots untied, rifle wrong. The sergeant spotted him with surprise at first, then chased him across the pavement, yelling, "Magna Para? Is that you, Magna Para? Am I dreaming, Magna Para? What is wrong with you, Magna Para? Everyone runs, you walk! Everyone lives, you gonna die! Do you understand me, Magna Para?"

Magna Para did this every time the whistle blew—same cards, same bluff. It nearly drove the sergeant insane. He'd push Magna Para, throw him to the ground, kick him in the ribs, but he always got up smiling. One night, because of Magna Para, the platoon had to get dressed and down the stairs fifteen times. Magna Para was given a spoon and told to crawl beneath the barracks and dig his own grave. They could hear him whistling to himself as he worked down there. One morning they woke up and Magna Para was gone—gear cleared out, locker empty. No explanation. It was as if Magna Para had never existed.

Herbie did see Magna Para once more. It was in the woods a few weeks after basic, miles from the barracks. Members of the platoon were taking part in an elaborate war game. "I heard someone calling me," Herbie said, "and I'm thinking, who the hell knows me way the hell out here, and I look over, and there, in a cage in a clearing, in a weird kind of prison cell, is Magna Para, only he doesn't seem to know he's in a cage. He's just happy to see us. He says, 'Hey, guys! How ya doing?'"

Magna Para was the first holy fool Herbie ever met, but would not be the last. He turned over his example and his reaction to power for the rest of his army days and for the rest of his life. Magna Para unintentionally taught Herbie that weakness can be strength, and ignorance, feigned or real, can be the best response to authority. Magna Para lived in our lives as a legend, something to think of at bedtime, but, as with most of Herbie's stories, we were meant to take away a serious lesson: the fool knows something hidden from the wise man.

No. 10

"WE WAITED ANXIOUSLY FOR OUR DEPLOYMENT ORDERS," Herbie told me. "It was like the lottery, only in this lottery you could also lose. Being sent to Korea—that was losing. Or some flyspeck Arctic atoll. Japan was a mixed bag, a good hitch but a little too close to the fighting. If Korea blew up into World War III, the guys in Japan would be the first to go."

Herbie drew a ticket to the European theater—a winner. He'd be part of the U.S. occupation forces that have been in Europe since the Nazi surrender in 1945. Of course, there was danger there, too. If the Russians invaded the West, as many expected, America's European soldiers would be in the thick of the fighting.

Herbie was flown to New York, then loaded on a troop carrier anchored in the Hudson. When the carrier passed through the Narrows, he could smell Brooklyn, hot dogs, baked goods, and grease. It was ten days across, a week and a half of swaying in his bunk, lining up for meals, staring at the sea. There was a mid-ocean squall, the ship tossed like a cork. He felt weak when he disembarked in Bremerhaven, a German port on the North Sea. He lived in a base in town while awaiting his next set of orders. He hoped to be stationed in France. He imagined walking the streets of Paris, a desk job, wine in a café at night. He'd taken classes in business administration at Camp Chaffee and had been accordingly classified "Clerk/Typist.".

When a sergeant asked if any of the men spoke a foreign language, Herbie raised his hand. He'd passed high school French and claimed he was fluent. It's not lying if you believe it. He spent a day taking language exams, which turned out to be the same day that service postings were selected and issued. Returning to the barracks, he learned that everyone had gotten an assignment but him. The ideal was to be posted in a big city, and, barring that, a small city, and, barring that, a large town. After learning he'd failed his French test, Herbie received his posting: a small town in central Germany called Bad Kissingen.

No one had heard of it.

He boarded a train with thousands of other soldiers. Most exited at the first few stops. Hannover, Göttingen, Northeim. Only a few dozen remained when the train reached Kassel, Germany. The sun was setting on the fields. The car was filled with pink light. Herbie stared out the window, thinking of his mother's family. They died in Poland. He drifted into a dreamless sleep. He woke with a start, jumped up in a panic, and went to find a conductor. They'd been traveling east for hours. How much farther could they go before crossing into the Soviet Union?

Several soldiers got off in Fulda, the last big town. The station had been destroyed in World War II. The ticket takers and bag handlers worked out of a temporary shelter while a new station was being built.

Herbie had to change trains in Würzburg. He waited in the dark with another soldier, a black private from Carthage,

Mississippi, then boarded a smaller train—a funicular—that took him farther east. The soldier from Mississippi got off in Schweinfurt, and Herbie continued alone to the last stop, the ancient resort town of Bad Kissingen. There were jeeps in the street, and a single artillery piece pointed at the sky.

For centuries, Bad Kissingen—"Bad K" to Americans—had been a summer retreat for German royals and aristocrats, a spa in a southern spur of the Rhön mountains. Bad K assumed military importance during the Cold War. Fulda was the best mountain pass from East Germany to West Germany. In the event of a war, the Russians would drive their tanks through the valley, which on military maps, circled in red and marked off with arrows, was identified as the Fulda Gap. In short, Herbie, who dreamed of a posting in the 13th arrondissement, found himself at ground zero of the coming apocalypse.

The border ran through the fields east of town. You couldn't miss it for the barbed wire, pillboxes, and gun towers. A patrol road was trafficked by every sort of armored vehicle. The Soviets had the Americans tremendously outgunned at Bad K, with thousands of Russian tanks stationed across the line. The GIs in these forward units—the front line of America's European army—served as a kind of human trip wire. They were not expected to stop the Soviets but to merely slow them down, giving the Allies time to mobilize. Most training at the Fulda Gap was in guerrilla tactics, because, in the event of war, the men stationed there would soon be dead or behind enemy lines.

Herbie was confused by the posting. Did someone have it in for him? Had he pissed off the wrong lieutenant?

There were no more than two hundred Americans at Bad Kissingen, all of them, except Herbie, from the Deep South. They were tankers, sharpshooters, demolition men. He spoke with a higher-up the next morning, explaining himself by showing his papers and saying, "There's been a mistake. I don't belong here. I'm a clerk/typist."

This man stapled a new page on top and said, "Your classification has been changed."

"To what?"

"Weasel Driver."

He'd been assigned to operate the rear gun of a half-track—a Weasel—that patrolled the border. He sat behind the big cannon, finger on the trigger guard, barrel pointed at the sky, a new member of Alabama's Twenty-Third Infantry. He was the only soldier from New York in Alabama's Twenty-Third, the only Sinatra lover, the only sophisticate. "No, no anti-Semitism," he said later. "They didn't even know what a Jew was."

In the barracks, he slept between a guitar-playing yokel— sixty years later, he still catches himself singing "I Dreamed of a Hillbilly Heaven"—and a bed wetter who cried after Taps. Everyone ignored the kid, but Herbie sat with him, talked to him, and asked him what was wrong. The kid confided to Herbie: he'd lied about his age to the enlistment officer. "I'm only fourteen years old," he whimpered. "I want to go home."

Herbie brought the kid to the Commanding Officer, a man Herbie refers to only as the Colonel, and explained the situation. Two days later, the kid was gone. That's how Herbie met the man—the Colonel—who'd raise him to a position of importance. It was the Colonel who later put Herbie in charge of "Courts and Boards," the unit that oversaw trial and punishment on the base. It was often Herbie alone who'd decide who was arrested and who was freed at Bad K, who was sent to Leavenworth and who went home, all because he'd been the only grunt decent enough to sit with the bed wetter and ask, "What's wrong?"

It was not the East Germans who worried Herbie on the border, but some of his fellow Americans, crazy rednecks who'd declare their intention to "kill a Commie," then shoot up the border fence or stitch an enemy tower with rifle shells. Several soldiers kicked five bucks a week into a pool to be awarded to the first man to "kill a Commie." Now and then, East Germans returned fire, turning what began as a boast into a gunfight. Herbie would crawl under the Weasel on such occasions, cursing as bullets punctured his tires. An exchange of messages would follow, the situation de-escalate, the incident appear in the local papers as a "minor clash," the sort not uncommon on hostile frontiers.

The army brass was at first amused, then annoyed, then concerned. Esprit de corps is one thing, but the hotheads of Alabama's Twenty-Third seemed intent on starting World War III. What do you do when the drink is too strong? Add ice or a mixer, which, for Bad Kissingen, was a brigade of soldiers from New York's Eighth Infantry. These men arrived ten months after Herbie, hundreds of grunts from Brooklyn, Long Island, Westchester, and Putnam County. The barracks filled with the sound of Johnny Mathis and the aroma of drugstore cologne. Herbie was greatly relieved by this development. It meant he wasn't going to die in Germany.

Herbie's best friend in those years, an army buddy right out of an old episode of *I Love Lucy*, arrived with the Eighth

Infantry. His name was Tommy DeLuca, and he was a tough little pug from Gun Hill Road in the Bronx. We heard about Tommy DeLuca throughout our childhood—another Tommy DeLuca story!—but did not meet him until thirty years after my father was discharged. Tommy DeLuca had been searching for Herbie for decades, calling every Herbert, Herbie, Herb, and H. Cohen in every big-city phone book in America. In 1996, he finally dialed the right number. When he introduced himself, my mother, who had met DeLuca a few times in New York in the early 1960s, screamed, "Tommy!"

He was carrying an old photo when he came to visit. It showed Herbie and a bunch of other soldiers at a German night club at closing time. My father reclines in a black-and-white-checked short-sleeve shirt, a cigarette glued to his lip in the manner of Robert Mitchum. Tommy is at his side, coat and tie, chin down, eyes focused on the camera. The table is covered with bottles and cocktail glasses. You can almost hear the laughter. You can almost smell the cigarette smoke. "That's me and your pop," DeLuca said, as if he could hardly believe it himself. "That's how we used to be."

That was the best time of Tommy DeLuca's life. There was neither muddle, gray area, nor confusion. He knew exactly when to get up and when to go to sleep, how to dress and what to do. He formed a club in Bad K, an invitation-only organization he called the Waste. As president of the Waste, DeLuca scouted and recruited members and appointed chairmen and officers. He devised rituals, too, secret handshakes and secret knocks, secret symbols and insignia and an esoteric initiation ceremony—here is the candle, here is the feather, here is the skull; do you agree to place this brotherhood before all others?

DeLuca made and enforced club rules—the Waste Man's Code—which were written in a book and hidden in his locker. In the back of the book, he'd written the name and rank of each member of the club. There were soon more than a hundred.

The Waste had no agenda and no purpose—not at first, anyway. It was just about having fun and wasting time, hence the name. There were parties, basketball games, drunken sprees. It was only when DeLuca began initiating army officers and MPs that membership came to have privileges. If a Waste Man was working at the base's gate, the secret handshake could get you in or out of town without a pass. If a Waste Man was in charge of leave, the secret code could get you a few extra days of R&R. It was a wheel within a wheel, a hub with a command structure that mirrored and seemed to mock that of the army. Private First Class Tommy DeLuca, powerless by day, controlled sergeants and lieutenants by night. It was Mardi Gras, where the servants are the masters from dusk until dawn and the peasants eat from silver trays.

When asked to join the Waste, Herbie politely turned DeLuca down. Herbie has had a lifelong aversion to private clubs and secret organizations. In this, he says, he has followed a precedent established by the founder of his family, Aaron, the brother of Moses and the first Hebrew priest. He told me that Aaron, having been approached by a group in the Sinai and asked to join a fraternal brotherhood much like the Elks—"only instead of an elk," says Herbie, "it was a golden calf"—refused the invitation, "establishing the tradition we've followed ever since."

"And what is the golden calf?" Herbie continues. "It's

everything that's not God. It's everything that takes you away from what matters. Money, cars, houses at the beach—it's all the golden calf. And the Waste was the golden calf, too."

Herbie wouldn't have had time for the Waste anyway. He'd been transferred from the border patrol to Courts and Boards, where he'd head the unit that investigated criminal activity on the base, file reports and suggest which cases to try and which to dismiss. It was work that gave him a rare insight into people—what made them tick, how they functioned under pressure, how some remained stoic and strong while others wept and told on their friends. It taught him how to spot mannerisms, tics that indicate a lie or bluff. "Those who can live with ambiguity and still function do the best," he told me. "Those who can't stand uncertainty get their certainty, but pay for it."

He still talks about some of the cases. The soldier who'd been refused service at the local tavern because he was slurring and belligerent. He stormed out, then returned in a Sherman tank, pushed the 120-millimeter cannon through the window, trained the barrel on the bartender, popped out of the hatch, and asked, "May I please have a beer?" Or the soldier—Balzano—who, in the middle of lunch in the mess hall, looked at his friends in confusion, and then started shouting, "Who are you? Where's my money? Where's my mama's milk?" Balzano said he didn't know where he was or how he got there. "Germany? Yeah, right. Go to hell." As he explained it to Herbie in the investigation, the last thing he remembered before waking in the strange mess hall was his mother giving him a nickel and sending him out for milk. Next he knows he's in this itchy green uniform, surrounded by soldiers who have apparently taken his nickel or his milk or both. Everyone assumed Balzano was bullshitting, playing the head case so he'd be sent home, but the doctors weren't sure and the soldiers couldn't break him. Balzano stayed in character even after his discharge papers had been signed. He was still at it on the way to the station, glaring at his friends and the MPs, saying, "Where's my money? Where's my mama's milk?" Then, after he was seated in the carriage with his duffel in his lap and the train had started to move, he turned, looked out the window, and smiled.

No. 11

HERBIE PLAYED A LOT OF BASKETBALL AT BAD KISSINGEN. There were two courts on base—an outside court bathed in floodlight and an inside court with bleachers and a scoreboard. Having made a study of the game in Brooklyn, Herbie deepened what he'd learned in the service. He liked basketball in Bensonhurst, but came to love it in Germany. The game felt like more than a game when he was overseas; it felt like home. It was the prose of Brooklyn translated into the poetry of sport. Whatever happens in life can be seen in miniature on the court. Whatever is true here will be just as true there; what is false here will lead to ruin there. Five players to a side is ideal for teamwork; five members is a military unit, a jazz band, a street gang. Five good players working together will always beat five great players working apart.

Herbie was a regular in the three-on-three games in the gym, where players followed the Brooklyn playground rules:

make it, take it; no harm, no foul; one point per hoop; first to ten; win by two; winner keeps the court.

The Colonel staged a three-on-three tournament twice a year. Herbie entered one of these tournaments with two friends from the barracks. Herbie was a good player, but not very good. His gifts were intellectual. He was what they used to call "heady," meaning more brain than brawn. He did a lot of talking on court. He was a solid defender and played on the edge of dirty. He did not want to injure an opponent, but would if absolutely necessary. His best shot was an old-fashioned hook. There was a spot from which he did not miss—ten feet out on the right side. He played point guard in the tournament, bringing the ball across mid-court, then initiating the offense with a pass. His team over-performed, knocking off several favorites. Herbie coached as well as played. He devised the strategy. Even then he believed that sport is really about tempo. If you prevent your opponent from playing at their preferred tempo, they'll become frustrated and you can win. If the other team is fast, make them play slow. If the other team is slow, make them play fast.

Herbie's team reached the final, where they faced what amounted to the Bad Kissingen all-stars, a squad led by "Famous Jimmy" Longo, the Bob Cousy of the German border. Though they'd never spoken, Herbie had tremendous admiration for Famous Jimmy—his size and speed, his power on the boards, his accuracy from outside.

The championship was played on a Friday night. If the Russians wanted to invade, that would have been the time. The patrol towers were half-staffed; the Weasels sat idle. Everyone was at the gym.

The game was surprisingly tight. Smaller, weaker, and not nearly as athletic, Herbie's team slowed the pace to a crawl, keeping the score low and close enough for Nate Feinstein—he later became an Ivy League law professor—to hit a go-ahead jumper with three seconds left.

Pandemonium.

A player on the other team, hurrying to get down court, threw the ball out of bounds, giving Herbie's team the final possession.

Herbie called a time-out.

"We make one inbound pass," he said, "and it's over."

Herbie decided he should inbound the ball, not because he was his team's best player—he was probably the worst—but because he believed himself the smartest, thus the least likely to make a mental error. He dried his hands on his shorts, took the ball from the referee, stepped to the sideline, and waved the ball over his head, looking for an open man. He spotted a player streaking down court, waving his arms, shouting, "Herbie! Herbie! I'm open."

Herbie wheeled and threw, delivering a bullet, a perfect pass, which the player caught and shot in a single motion. Swish. It was only later—a long moment later, when the people in the seats started laughing—that Herbie realized he had thrown the ball to Famous Jimmy, who'd won the championship with the last shot.

What do you do after such a monumental mistake?

Do you curse and spit and kick the ground and bang yourself on the skull and condemn God and the refs and the life that has brought you to this point?

Herbie was smiling when he got back to the bench.

He said, "I can't believe Famous Jimmy knows my name!"

He said, "That was probably the best pass I've ever thrown. It had to be perfect to beat the clock."

No. 12

THE COLONEL SUMMONED HERBIE EARLY THE NEXT MORN-ing. This was unusual, even scary. Colonels don't summon privates unless something has gone terribly wrong. Herbie's mind was racing as he walked across the parade ground.

What did I screw up? he asked himself.

But the Colonel greeted him with a handshake and a smile, saying, "That was a hell of an effort yesterday.

"In fact," he added, "that's what I want to talk to you about."

The best basketball players in the American military competed in two European leagues, the alpha league and the beta league. The teams in the beta league represented companies and battalions; a battalion could include as many as two hundred soldiers, a company as many as a thousand. These teams consisted of playground and high school standouts. Some would go on to play at small colleges. The teams in the alpha league represented brigades and divisions; a brigade could include as many as five thousand soldiers, a company as many as fifteen thousand. The players in the alpha league were top level. Some would play at schools like Ohio State, Notre Dame, Michigan. A handful would go on to play or coach in the NBA.

The Colonel understood the nature of Herbie's accomplishment in the three-on-three tournament, how he'd taken the least talented team to the final by devising a strategy, teaching his players, and getting them to stick to it, greatly outperforming their ability. "I don't know how you did it, Cohen, but you managed to squeeze sixty pounds into a ten-pound sack."

He asked Herbie if he could do the same with Bad Kissingen's battalion team, a perennial beta league loser. There was a scarcity of athletic talent on the border. "I'm not asking you to win a championship," said the Colonel, who functioned as the team's general manager. "I'd just like to be competitive."

From that moment until his military discharge, Herbie had one job: coaching basketball. He organized tryouts. He was familiar with most of the players on base but wanted to see them again—in new situations, with different teammates. And, of course, there's always the chance of a discovery, a diamond in the dirt. He started with Famous Jimmy, a six-foot-five forward from Baton Rouge, Louisiana, then surrounded him with specialists, assembling the team in the way of an elite unit from a World War II mission movie—this one because he's devastating from twenty feet, that one because he sets a vicious pick, this one because he's all elbows and Nietzschean will, that one because he intuits the flow of the game. There was Sam Jones, a six-foot-four white guard who'd later play at Holy Cross; Bobby Morgan, a six-foot-seven black center who'd later play professionally in Italy; Fats Portnoy, a five-foot-seven Jewish guard who later became a legendary high school coach; and Bobby Whitefeather a six-foot-five Cherokee forward who'd later play for a Native American Tribal college.

Herbie ran preseason practice four nights a week. He spent the rest of his time on the road, traveling base to base, ducking into gyms, standing in the back of the bleachers, taking notes as he watched the opposition, writing down names, numbers, tendencies. Bad Kissingen would indeed be outgunned. Being in the Fulda Gap meant putting military need ahead of basketball. Unlike battalions farther from the front, the Colonel could not recruit soldiers with only sports in mind. As a result, Bad K did not match up on court. Even Famous Jimmy, the base superstar, would have been no more than average on most of the other teams in the beta league.

Herbie accordingly devised a strategy aimed less at elevating his team than at degrading—slowing, frustrating, mucking up—the competition, turning the games into slogs from which Bad K would emerge with a victory like a junkyard dog with a bone. "Those we can't beat," explained Herbie, "we can get to beat themselves."

Bad K played like geriatrics that season, at wheelchair or walker speed, passing, passing, passing, passing. They'd slow each moment to what felt like an eternity, then live in that eternity. It drove opposing players crazy. They'd lash out, jump into the lane, go for impossible steals, get into foul trouble. Or else the pace would make them sleepy. They'd lose interest, forget why they'd come. By the end of the second half, they'd be hypnotized—eyes getting heavier and heavier, and here is a soft green meadow, and wouldn't it be lovely to lie down in the cool grass? At the crucial instant, Bad K would flip on the burners—a fast break, an end-to-end pass, a layup, steal, or fadeaway jumper—scoring just enough to win. Or they'd shift speed, go from fast to slow, then back, keeping the opposition off balance in the way of a junk ball pitcher.

The team spent the winter on trains and buses, crisscrossing West Germany. Würzburg, Heidelberg, Stuttgart, Worms, Wiesbaden, Limburg, Zweibrücken, Saarbrücken. The intimacy of the run-down arenas, the sound of sneakers on hardwood floors, country roads, medieval churches and greens, the forest beyond the last streetlight, nights when it rained, nights when it snowed, clear nights filled with stars, the industrial zones, factories and smokestacks, the somber infrastructure, the camaraderie of the team, Americans together in a foreign land where toilets flush with a chain and rubble from the war is still piled in the squares.

"Was it strange?" I asked my father.

"Was what strange?"

"Being a Jew in Germany so soon after the Holocaust."

"Just once it was strange," he said. "I'd spent the night at the house of a German girl. We'd been out drinking, and before I knew it, it was too late to go back to base. I had an overnight pass, anyway, so I slept at her parents' house in a guest room. When I came down in the morning, I saw a picture of her father on the mantel. He was posed in uniform. I leaned close and studied it. Son of a bitch. He'd been a colonel in the SS. But, you know what, we'd won the war, we'd beat the Nazi bastards, and that meant everything."

The Bad K team finished 18 and 12, which put them in the playoffs. A single elimination tournament: two victories got you to the final. There was a party on the base the night before they left. Most of the players were hungover when the train reached Düsseldorf, where the games would be played in a gym in the center of town.

Herbie dressed like a civilian on the bench, in suit and tie, a cigar ready for the postgame celebration. His picture occasionally appeared in *The Stars and Stripes*, which covered the beta league. He looks skinny in some, chubby in others. His eyes are pale, his face is dark, his brow is furrowed. He coaches with his hands, moving players this way and that. He writes on the sideline, filling a slate with dots and dashes. No matter the situation, he has a plan. No matter the trouble, a solution. No matter the riddle, a story to tell. "You have nothing to lose," he told his players before the final. "If you fail, you're doing what everyone expects. But if you win . . . think of how embarrassed the guys across the floor will be!"

The first game was punctuated by hard fouls and shoving. It was slow, ugly. And Bad K won. The second was even uglier. The opposing coach, an airborne commander stationed in Frankfurt, accused Herbie of playing "tricky New York ball." Herbie responded by giving him the finger with both hands, the so-called double bird. This led to a melee, at the end of which Herbie was ejected. The crowd booed when they realized Herbie had been kicked out while the airborne commander was allowed to stay. Herbie put Longo in charge, then stood in the hallway that led to the court. Now and then, a Bad K player would walk off the court and through the door, then return. The airborne commander complained that Herbie was coaching "by proxy." The referee went into the hall, found Herbie, and ordered him to go to the locker room and stay there.

Bad K won on the last shot, a layup off a rebound by Longo. This put Bad K in the final, but Herbie, as per referee decision, would not be allowed to coach. He went to the game as a fan, bought a ticket, and sat in the bleachers, where his players sought his direction, which he shouted through cupped hands, a strange spectacle that was chronicled, in words and photos, by *The Stars and Stripes*: Fats Portnoy and Bobby Whitefeather standing at the bottom of the seats, looking up, listening. Herbie was accused of "coaching from the stands." The referees did nothing at first. Then, in the second half, they told him to stay seated and stop talking. He did, but the opposing coach told the referees that Herbie was using hand and eye signals to direct players. Herbie was told to leave the arena. When he protested—"Secret signals? Who does he think I am? 'The Amazing Randi'?"—the MPs were summoned. *The Stars and Stripes* ran a picture of Herbie being led out of the arena by armed men. Bad K, unsettled by the spectacle, lost the game by ten points.

No. 13

HERBIE WAS SUMMONED BY THE COLONEL A FEW DAYS AFter he'd returned to the base. The Colonel was talking with a thick-set general when Herbie came in. The General had been at the beta league tournament. He was a basketball fanatic, Indiana born and raised, and, as such, had made himself the sponsor of the Second Cavalry's alpha league team. He'd pulled strings and called in favors to load the squad with talent, yet they underperformed and were in danger of not even making the playoffs. They'd have to win six of their last ten games to avoid regular-season elimination. "And elimination, I have no need to tell you, Private Cohen, is humiliation. And I will not have those stuffed shirts at headquarters laughing at me." Having fired his coach—a captain from a mechanized unit—the General ordered Herbie to take over the team and "salvage what can be saved."

Herbie traveled to Frankfurt to see the team the next day. As he watched them lose to a clearly inferior squad, one thing was obvious: the Second Cavalry, though indeed talented, had hardly been coached. There was little passing, no creativity. It was every man for himself out there, which made for a slow game—listless, mechanical—though not in a purposeful way. They played a half-court offense and did not run on defense, as if they were bored, going through the motions. It was the kind of elegant lassitude you get from great athletes who have stopped caring. Lions in repose, dozing in the tall grass.

Herbie took over in Berlin. He said nothing for the first few games, but merely sat on the bench, taking notes. (For my father, taking notes is key—everywhere, all the time—because it lets you learn from the past, lets you keep a record while letting the other side know that a record is being kept, and, on occasion, lets you "hang them with their own words.")

He watched his team lose in Stuttgart and Mannheim, then called them together before the next practice. He'd devised a strategy based on the skills and deficiencies of each player. It was still tempo he was interested in, only now, after watching the Second Cav in games and practice, it was speed he wanted: play fast, race up and down the court. "You can't build a team around a random strategy," he explained decades later. "Maybe in a perfect world, heaven or fantasyland, but in the real world you have to devise your strategy for the talent you actually have. Don't bitch. Don't complain. Just play the cards you've been dealt. You think I wanted to play slow, play ugly, watch my boys slog in the mire? Of course not! But that was the only way Bad K could compete. We weren't good, so we had to make the other teams play worse than us. But the Second Cav had talent, which meant we could play fast. You can teach a person to pass and set a pick, but you can't teach speed. That's God given."

He designed his offense around the fast break, transition being the order of the day: get the ball down court more quickly than the defense can follow. When the Second Cav took possession, the guard whipped the ball to mid-court, where another guard caught it, turned, and threw it to a forward breaking for the basket. On occasion, the ball went end to end without touching the floor. It was all about teamwork, anticipation, pinpoint passing, which takes practice, repetition. There were miscues, overthrows, and underthrows in those first games, blown assignments, but when it clicked, the Second Cav became a force in the alpha league. They won several games in a row at the end of the season, then continued winning in the playoffs. They blew out every team in the early rounds and made it to the final, where they faced a Seventh Army squad composed entirely of ringers, including Larry Costello, who'd play and coach in the NBA, where he made six all-star teams.

The final was held in a rickety stadium in central France. The rafters creaked when the wind blew. The seats on the floor were jammed with military brass. It seemed as if every general and colonel in Europe had turned out in dress blues. Privates and sergeants filled the bleachers, where cigarette smoke lingered. Herbie's center, Bobby Watkins of Albuquerque, New Mexico, a rangy cowboy, went out for the opening tip. The ref blew a whistle, made the toss. Going after it, the players hung in the air for what felt like an age, their arms reaching for a ball that paused between ascent and descent, the crowd, the noise, teammates waiting, coaches prowling, the hardwood shine, all of it frozen in a photographer's magnesium flare.

The game was a barn burner, the lead changing hands a dozen times. It was tied with two seconds left. The Second Cav had possession at mid-court. Herbie signaled for timeout. Here was the question: Is it even possible to score in two seconds? Herbie called a play the team had been working on. The ref handed the ball to the Second Cav's point guard, who stood on the sideline, looking to inbound. The two guards raced back as if to receive a pass. The point guard faked, turned, and threw up court toward the hoop, where Bobby Watkins, the rangy cowboy, met the ball in the air—starting the clock—then redirected it off the backboard and into the basket for the win. A primordial version of the alley-oop, the play sent the spectators out of their seats and onto the floor in celebration. Herbie drank champagne in the locker room, then continued on to a local saloon for a party that lasted from can till can't.

No. 14

HE WAS BLEARY WHEN HE WALKED INTO THE BARRACKS AT Bad Kissingen the next morning. He'd expected rapturous congratulations, but everyone was downcast. Something had happened; he could feel it as soon as he stepped through the door. It woke him up in a moment.

"What's going on?" he asked, dumping his bag on his bunk.

"It's DeLuca," said Nate Feinstein. "They took him away."

"What do you mean? Who took him away?"

"The MPs."

Nate Feinstein looked around, then continued in a whisper: "Two guys in black suits came in here yesterday, broke into DeLuca's trunk and locker, spread all his stuff out on the floor, and took pictures of everything with this tiny little camera."

"Where's Tommy now?"

"In the brig. I tried to see him; they wouldn't let me."

Herbie went directly to the brig, a concrete jailhouse in the center of the base. It had to be about the Waste, he told himself. He figured DeLuca had broken some ordinance by mixing officers and enlisted men and faced a charge on rule violations. Herbie was right, and wrong. It was about the Waste, only it wasn't a rule violation. DeLuca had been charged with treason.

Herbie figured he could use his position at Courts and Boards to bluff his way in to see DeLuca, but was wrong about that, too. Private First Class DeLuca was being kept under armed guard in isolation; you'd have to be at least a captain to get in.

Stopping near the door that led to the cells, Herbie called back, "Hey, Tommy? You in there?"

"Herbie, is that you? I'm in trouble, Herbie."

"I know, Tommy."

"You got to help me, Herbie."

"Don't worry," Herbie said. "We're going to fix this."

For Herbie, it was Moppo turning up at the assembly all over again. There was a mess, a misunderstanding, a crisis, but what is a mess, a misunderstanding, and a crisis but a game, a puzzle in want of a solution?

He started the next morning, talking to every officer in the chain of command, working his way up the ranks until he found himself back in the office of the Colonel, who agreed to talk about the case only after Herbie had given him the blow-by-blow of the alpha league final.

"Now for your friend," said the Colonel, who'd had his secretary retrieve the file.

The Colonel grimaced as he read through it, muttering, "Jesus Christ" and "Great God Almighty."

"This looks bad," the Colonel said. "They're going to send

him to Leavenworth. Once upon a time, he would have been stood against a wall and shot for this."

"I don't understand. What did he do?"

The Colonel described the Waste as it appeared to the military: Private First Class DeLuca formed a secret subversive organization on the East German border, recruited officers into that organization, placed those officers beneath enlisted men in a separate command structure, undermining military readiness at the Fulda Gap with probable intent to aid the enemy.

A Russian spy had apparently infiltrated the Waste, written reports on DeLuca's secret meetings, copied DeLuca's rule book and roster, and carried it all back to Russian intelligence, who leaked it to the Soviet press. The Waste made *Pravda*, where it was reported as evidence of dissent within the U.S. Army.

Herbie laughed when he heard this, then stopped laughing. Over the next few days, he made it his mission to prove that *Pravda* and the Russians were wrong, that DeLuca could not possibly have organized such a plot, because, as Herbie put it, "Tommy DeLuca is an idiot."

Herbie explained this first to the Colonel, then to the officer who ran army intelligence on the border, making the case that punishing DeLuca would do more harm than good. "The Russians think they've exposed this big plot," Herbie explained. "If you prosecute DeLuca, you'll prove them right. And they win. But if you show DeLuca to be the idiot we all know him to be, you'll make the Russians look like fools."

Having noticed a stuffed largemouth bass on the wall behind the intelligence officer's desk, and believing that people best understand solutions phrased in their own language, Herbie went on: "The Russians think they've hooked a marlin. They're bragging about it. If you charge DeLuca with treason, you'll tell everyone they're right and there is a problem in the American army. But if you charge him for what he actually did—act like an idiot—then everyone will see that the Russians caught a tire but they're such fools they've put it on their wall and are telling everyone it's a marlin."

When the criminal report was released, DeLuca had been accused of nothing more than insubordination. He was knocked down to private and cashiered from the military. He'd been given an OTH, an "Other Than Honorable Discharge," which was not the best but also not the worst thing in the world. He wept in Herbie's arms when he returned to the barracks, then got dressed for a goodbye dinner at a local beer garden. He was leaving months ahead of his friends, disgraced and alone. Nietzsche said, "That which does not kill me makes me stronger," but this wasn't the case with Tommy DeLuca. The talk of treason scared him, and he stayed scared. He was still scared when I met him decades later. He became a regular presence in our lives in his later years. He was with us at Thanksgiving and Hanukah and on family vacations. He felt safe around Herbie. Herbie had rescued him once and, Tommy believed, could rescue him again.

No. 15

FOR MANY YEARS, HERBIE'S FAVORITE PIECE OF WRITING was "The Eighty-Yard Run" by Irwin Shaw. The story takes place in the mind of Christian Darling, a once promising youth who, having amounted to nothing, sits on a hill on the campus of his old college, looking down at the football field, where he'd achieved the great success of his life, returning a kickoff eighty yards for a touchdown. It did not even happen in a game, but in practice, and yet, looking back, he can see that everything was downhill from there. That's what Herbie was afraid of at the end of his military service—that he'd just experienced his eighty-yard run and would never feel so at home in the world again.

He was discharged in October 1955. He'd known the end was near, yet it still came before he was ready. He spent his last weeks in uniform in a funk. He'd been a great success in the army, had found his place, earned his privileges. Who's to say he'd ever be so accomplished again? Maybe Bad Kissingen had been his eighty-yard run.

He did not want anyone to meet his ship in New York, nor even know his date of return. He planned to slip into Brooklyn, creep in through a side door, and be waiting at the kitchen table when his parents woke up for breakfast. But that's not what happened. Larry, who'd felt rudderless without Herbie, had been calling the military's family outreach office twice a week to ask when Private Cohen would return, on what ship, at what pier.

Larry told Herbie's parents when he got the information, and the three of them—Morris, Esther, Larry—were waiting at Pier 32 when Herbie, a duffel bag thrown over his shoulder, walked down the gangplank into Manhattan.

Larry and Esther talked all the way home. Morris, who was driving, concentrated on the road. Herbie stared out the window—at the West Side Highway, then at the Brooklyn-

Battery Tunnel, then at the stores along Hamilton Avenue in Brooklyn. Twentieth Street led to Bay Parkway, which was candy shops, taverns, playgrounds, and street corners all the way back to what Herbie describes as "picturesque Bensonhurst on serene Gravesend Bay, where we played little-league polo and fished bodies from the icy waters of the Gowanus Canal."

No. 16

HERBIE SPENT HIS FIRST WEEKS BACK HOME WITH OLD friends on the corner, trying to be as he had been, but it was not long before he understood it was impossible. Almost all his friends had left Brooklyn, or were preparing to go.

The Italian futurist Umberto Boccioni painted a triptych called *States of Mind.* The first work shows the people we have left behind, stranded and aimless in green light. The second work shows the machinery of travel, steam engines, traffic lights, smoke. The third work shows the dislocation of those who have left home, the chaos, hope, and regret, because once you leave, you can never return. Your first world vanishes as soon as you step out the door.

Bensonhurst was like that in the 1950s. You were either gone, going, or had been left behind. Zeke had gotten married while Herbie was in Germany. When Herbie asked why he'd married a person he did not even seem to like—her name was Frada—Larry said, "Because you were in the army, and it was winter, and I was bored." Who Ha had moved to Long Island, where he worked as something called a "manufacturer's representative" and married a woman named Honey. Sandy had signed a contract with the Dodgers and would soon make his Ebbets Field debut. Asher Dann, another friend from the corner, had moved to L.A., where, because of good looks alone, he had been signed by Twentieth Century Fox. Asher made a single movie, the 3-D classic *September Storm*, in which he appears as the nearly always shirtless cabin boy Manuel Del Rio Montoya.

Herbie returned to NYU. He was still living at home and commuting to the Greenwich Village campus, but went at it with a new sense of purpose. His military service—boot camp at Camp Chaffee, riding a Weasel in the Fulda Gap, coaching basketball in the European League—had focused him. And he was not the only one. There were hundreds of veterans at NYU, men attending college on the GI Bill. They were older than the other students, more experienced and more mature, sharks among minnows. Herbie's crowd lingered in the Cedar Tavern after class, talking about world affairs and domestic politics. Most preferred *The New York Times* to the *Daily News*, Adlai Stevenson to Dwight Eisenhower, wine to beer. Having worn his high school letterman's jacket—he'd been a backup tackle on the football team—or his Warriors colors before the army and an olive-green uniform during, Herbie began turning up for class in suits or sport coats, dark in summer, pastel in spring, hair slicked back, clean shaven and ready.

He majored in English and history, his sights fixed on law school. He believed that no matter what happens to a person's dreams, a lawyer will always "have something to fall back on." In a bigger sense, he was adrift, waiting for whatever or whoever it was that would give his life direction to appear. It's at this age, in this mood, that men join motorcycle gangs, concoct universal theories of matter, and develop a passion for poetry or computer programming.

My father met my mother instead.

My parents told different stories about their first meeting, or maybe it was the same story told in different ways, filtered through different sensibilities.

Ellen says it happened in the NYU cafeteria on Washington Square in the spring of 1957. She was eating lunch with friends before an afternoon class. Herbie walked in, scanned the room, caught her eye, came over, sat down. He knew one of the girls slightly. Looking first at this girl, then at Ellen, he said, "Has anyone seen Marty Eisenberg? I need to borrow his Econ notes."

This was a lie. There was no Marty Eisenberg—Herbie made up the name—and did not take Econ. He wanted to meet Ellen. She was a nineteen-year-old freshman, clever and pretty with short dark hair. They started talking and were soon deep in conversation. They were still talking after the room had cleared out and Ellen had missed her class.

Ellen later said she'd fallen in love with Herbie as soon as he sat down. The girls of her generation were raised on the myth of romantic love—"at first sight," "you just know," "one person forever"—and willed such moments into existence accordingly.

She went home that night and told her father she'd met the man she was going to marry.

"Do you love him, Ellen?"

"I sure do, Pop."

Pointing at his eyes, heart, then crotch, he said, "Is it here, here, or here?"

"It's all of those places, Pop."

Herbie's version is more fantastic. Ellen was sensible, committed to the literal truth. To Herbie, there is truth, and then there is *truth*, or, as he says, "You see things not as they are, but as you are." He believes in founding myths and fairy tales, in giving people a story, a poetic reality that supersedes the facts on the ground.

Or it can just be his love of bullshit.

He says it rained the day he met Ellen. Then the rain stopped and the sky cleared and a rainbow appeared over Manhattan. He followed it down Twelfth Street, through the doors, and into the NYU cafeteria, where he first saw Ellen.

"You understand what I'm telling you," he'd say. "I found your mother at the end of a rainbow."

Ellen commuted to school from Midwood, Brooklyn, where she lived with her parents, Ben and Betty Eisenstadt, her big sister, Gladys, also an NYU student, and her little brother, Ira. Her older brother, Marvin, was married and living in an apartment on Ocean Parkway.

Ellen was handsome in a way prized by that Jewish generation: she did not look Jewish. "Look at her!" the great-aunts would say. "You'd never even know!"

Her features were delicate. She had long fingers, high cheekbones, and the all-time best laugh. She had the wounded quality of a pretty girl who believes herself ugly because that's what she's been told, most frequently by her sister, Gladys, who had suffered Ellen's birth as a personal rebuke, a wound that would never heal.

The summer of 1957 was the season of courtship for Herbie and Ellen, dinners downtown, Greenwich Village after midnight, subway rides, and cheap tickets to Broadway shows—*Damn Yankees*, *West Side Story*. And movies. The 1950s are often depicted as a dull decade, a time of repression and sublimation, Ike on the golf course, the man in the gray flannel suit, but that's not the whole story. America in the 1950s was as secure as it would ever be, but anxiety was coming out of the rat holes. Frank Sinatra was still center stage, but Bob Dylan was in the wings, lunch counter sit-ins, civil rights, Sputnik, the missile gap, death from above. It could end at any moment, a hard rain, life snuffed out like a candle. It was all in the movies—*Vertigo*, *The Defiant Ones*, *Run Silent, Run Deep*—once you knew how to look.

If Ellen hadn't taken the initiative and kissed Herbie, it never would've happened. She did it on the Eisenstadts' front porch in Midwood. Herbie was startled. He didn't know what to do with his hands. He kissed the way actors kissed in movies, mouth closed, face jammed into hers. He called this a "soul kiss." When it was over, he said, "I think I might love you," turned, and ran.

Bensonhurst was just a few miles from Midwood, but it felt like another country. The apartment buildings and crowded stoops, pizza parlors and secondhand stores—it was working class, exotic. For Ellen, the relationship took on the thrill of the illicit. Ellen's world was just as strange to Herbie; she was upper middle class, a rich girl. She lived not in an apartment but in a house! She had a yard and a basement and an attic, and even her mother had been to college. There were times when Herbie looked at Ellen the way Gatsby looked at Daisy: the unattainable, the ladder that could take you above the clouds. There was a green light in the Eisenstadts' front parlor. Herbie swam for it.

Don't get me wrong. He loved his neighborhood and toured her through it with great pride. Eighty-Sixth and Bay Parkway, the JCH, the Warriors' clubhouse. He took her everywhere, introduced her to everyone. Inky, Bucko, Ben the Worrier, Gutter Rat—they did not make a favorable impression. To Ellen, these men were Neanderthals, goons.

Larry introduced himself as "Herbie's best friend."

Ellen liked him least of all; there was an emptiness behind his eyes, as if he had no inner life, as if he were only appetite.

"I don't trust him," she'd say.

Larry was married to his first wife at the time, Frada. He suggested some of the Warriors go as a group with their girlfriends or wives to see the hot new Broadway show *Carousel*. Because he had a job near Times Square, Larry offered to go to the box office. Pooling their cash, the friends handed Larry around eighty dollars, more than enough for ten tickets.

Larry led the couples through midtown the night of the show, then, when he should have taken a right, took a left instead.

"The theater is this way," said Inky's girlfriend, pointing down Fifty-Fifth Street.

"I know where I'm going," said Larry.

After much bickering and confusion, he led them to a run-down theater on the corner on Sixth Avenue. All hell broke loose when he handed out the tickets; they weren't for *Carousel* but for *Uncle Willie*, a Yiddish play featuring the vaudeville warhorse Menasha Skulnik. Larry had put the eighty dollars on the wrong horse, then scrounged up just enough cash to get seats to *Uncle Willie*.

Ellen would never forget it.

No. 17

HERBIE TOOK ELLEN TO MEET HIS PARENTS—MORRIS AND Esther—in August. Esther served a five-course meal on fine china in the small Bensonhurst dining room, where the windows looked out on a strip of red brick and a strip of black sky.

Esther was in her fifties, a short, shapely, gray-haired woman who could turn out a table of delicacies at the flip of a skirt. In Poland, the term for a person like this is *balabusta*, a nearly mythical creature who, according to Chabad.org, "can host twenty guests for Shabbat in an immaculately clean home, while keeping her kids entertained and well-behaved, simultaneously maintaining a calm composure and a perfectly clean outfit."

She'd arrived in America by herself at age fourteen, having been sent from Bielsk, Poland, to live with relatives in New York. She was meant to be followed by the rest of her family, but money was scarce, and the war came, and so she was possibly the only survivor, not just of her family, but of her town.

As the last of a species, she was determined to carry on its recipes, manners, and traditions. Esther served soup with *cliskels*, a delicious dumpling the likes of which have vanished from the earth, brisket, lemon cake, and black-and-white cookies from Bensonhurst's 18th Avenue Bakery.

Morris was a trickster, a pixie with white hair and flashing blue eyes. It would take Ellen years to be comfortable around him. She never knew when he was joking and could never guess what he was going to say. He'd made the trip from Poland twenty years before Esther. He settled first on the Lower East Side, where he worked in the garment industry, eventually making enough money to bring over the rest of his family, his brothers Itzhak and Nathan, his parents, Hannah and Noah. (Another brother, Moishe, had been kicked by a horse and killed in Poland.) Morris and Nathan opened a factory, a fifteen-man shop in SoHo that made bindings for the brims of fedoras, porkpies, bowlers—every kind of hat. The business would be devastated when John F. Kennedy began going around bareheaded.

Morris, who subscribed to a Yiddish newspaper, spoke with his hands, favored Democrats, and feared Communism, was semiretired by the time Ellen arrived on the scene. He spent most of his days with Esther, egging her on and reining her in. If not squeezing you with her warm soft hands, refilling your plate, refreshing your drink, wiping the schmutz off your face, fixing your collar, or wrapping food for you to take home, Esther was gossiping: talking up or tearing down. She could be as mean as Don Rickles, as cutting as Richard Pryor, explaining how this one was dumber than a box of hammers and that one was cold as a fish, taking thirty minutes to tell a story that could be summed up in a phrase, then saying, "That's it in a nutshell." Esther had no filter. If she thought it, she said it: "What happened? You used to be good-looking." "What happened? How did you get so fat?" Morris kept her worst tendencies in check. Laying a hand on her wrist, he'd say, "Enough, Esther. Enough."

For Ellen, Morris and Esther, though a bit inscrutable, were a blast of sea air. A flash of color, a taste of the lumpen proletariat, lower-middle-class life. While her own parents were well-mannered and soft-spoken and worried what people would think, Morris and Esther were warm and profane. They worried about everything and nothing. In this, they would turn out to be an embarrassment to Betty and Ben Eisenstadt, who hadn't climbed out of the old immigrant neighborhoods just to have Ellen pull them back in. Morris was only half-joking when he said, "The Eisenstadts covered the mirrors and said Kaddish when Ellen accepted Herbert's proposal. They considered it a mixed marriage, frowned upon by the community."

No. 18

FOR HERBIE, STEPPING THROUGH ELLEN'S DOOR WAS LIKE walking into the middle of a movie. He was immediately caught up in the drama, the emotional soap opera of the Eisenstadts, the sibling rivalries and godlike parents, the eleven-fingered maid, the scary basement and smell of mothballs, the screaming and broken dishes, the grandma, the dog, the arguments.

The house was at 3245 Avenue K in Midwood. There were

five bedrooms, a living room, a dining room, an eat-in kitchen. The front porch was shaded by a steel awning, and the house itself, which was deep and narrow with a pitched roof, sat amid a stretch of nearly identical brick houses. Approaching it was like entering an Escher drawing.

For Ellen's father, the house stood for success, his ascent into the middle class. As good as orphaned before his tenth birthday, Ben was passed from uncle to uncle until he was old enough to strike out on his own. He'd put himself through law school, then, not able to find legal work during the Great Depression, had taken a job as a counterman at a Red Hook diner, fallen for a waitress, Betty, who happened to be the owner's daughter, took over the diner, and moved it to a larger space at the corner of Cumberland Street and Flushing Avenue across from the Brooklyn Navy Yard, where business boomed in the run-up to World War II. For Ben, the move to Midwood was like a move to a posh suburb. He'd gone from an apartment in Red Hook, where hammers pound and steam whistles blast, to a house with its own driveway and yard. He raised his children in that house, Marvin, Gladys, and Ellen. Then Ira.

Ben was on the verge of greater success when Herbie arrived. He'd converted his diner into a packinghouse after the war. It was Ben Eisenstadt who, by taking apart and rebuilding a tea bag, invented the sugar packet, then went on to invent, among other things—he was a wispy-haired blue-eyed genius, a tinkerer, designer, and solver of problems—the soy sauce pack and the vacuum pack. By 1950, Cumberland was packing sugar for refineries, soy and duck sauce for wholesalers, and even fireworks.

But Ben wanted to be a creator. He wanted to fill his packets with his own products, his own elixirs. He also wanted to look good in a suit, as sleek as the men on the billboards. In 1954, he put these ideas together and came up with Sweet'N Low, which started as a fantasy of fake sugar, a way to sweeten your coffee without paying the price. Working with a chemist and his own son Marvin, Ben began concocting solutions—saccharine, cyclamate, cream of tartar—in search of the least unpalatable mix. He was, in addition to taste, after a quality described as "mouthfeel."

Picking Ellen up for a movie or a show or a basketball game, Herbie was often greeted by a table of coffee mugs, each sweetened with a slightly different Sweet'N Low formula. Herbie was told to sip from each, then decide which tasted the most like sugar. Decades later, when the FDA banned saccharine because it caused cancer in lab animals, Herbie's first response was "I knew that son of a bitch was trying to kill me."

No. 19

HERBIE AND ELLEN GOT MARRIED IN A BIG HALL ON OCEAN Parkway on June 23, 1957. Nearly everyone in the wedding pictures is now old or dead, even the kids. Some of the guests have been dead for sixty years. Ellen's sister—my aunt Gladys—either is missing from or looks angry in these photos. She claimed that it was not only strange but immoral and possibly evil for the little sister to get married first. Years later, long after she'd taken to her bed, Gladys said it was Ellen's marriage that caused her to give up on life.

Herbie and Ellen moved directly from the homes of their parents into an apartment together. Ellen, barely twenty, had never lived with anyone but immediate family members. She was pregnant by the spring of her junior year in college. Their daughter, Sharon, was born in the fall semester of her senior year. Herbie had graduated from college by then. He spent nights at NYU Law School and worked a variety of jobs during the day, eventually taking a full-time position at All-state Insurance. He started as a claims adjuster, a job that served as a kind of postgrad course in his lifelong study of negotiation. It was in these years, while establishing just how much the company should pay out for water damage, car wrecks, lightning strikes, and fires, that he began to turn what he'd done naturally on the street in Bensonhurst into a career.

Asked to define negotiation on the old *Tom Snyder* show, he said, "It's two kids arguing on the corner of Eighty-Sixth and Bay Parkway. It's a husband and wife fighting about where to have dinner. It's a mom getting her kid to do homework. It's John Kennedy talking to Khrushchev and Khrushchev banging his shoe on the table and screaming, 'We will bury you,' Khrushchev, who, all the while, has two perfectly good shoes on his feet. It's not something you learn, but something you've always known and have been doing all your life."

Herbie climbed like a rocket through the ranks at Allstate. He started in his car, driving accident to accident, examining damage, interviewing cops, firemen, experts, claimants, writing reports, determining settlements, then arguing about those determinations. By 1960, he'd been moved into an

office. As in the army, progress meant working indoors. He was put in charge of his own crew. He trained new hires, sent adjusters out on jobs, edited and occasionally rewrote reports, stepped in when a claim went sideways. He was the man in the financing shed, the wizard behind the curtain, the closer in the bullpen. He said a key to his success was settling quickly rather than fighting, overpaying a little instead of going to court and overpaying a lot—negotiation.

Because his crew outperformed all others, he was put in charge first of an office, then of a region. He was promoted four times in five years, each promotion meaning a new office in a new town. Between 1960 and 1965, Herbie and Ellen—who now had a son and a daughter—moved four times. They went from a one-bedroom apartment on Aurelia Court in

Brooklyn, to a three-bedroom house in Berkeley Heights, New Jersey, to a four-bedroom house in Syosset, Long Island. Every step was a step up, every move was a move forward—a bigger foyer, a flatter yard, a larger sky.

Sweet'N Low had been perfected by the time Herbie and Ellen exited Brooklyn. A pink packet had been chosen to stand out among the white packets of sugar, a logo had been designed, slogans invented and run in advertisements and printed on billboards. Ben, who'd started by distributing the product to pharmacies and health centers where it was presented as an alternative for diabetics and the obese, soon discovered there was a mainstream market for his elixir—a hunger, a need. Modern advertising had made nearly everyone feel the same way about their bodies—not good. If you wanted the taste but hated the shame, the mirror, the way your clothes chafed, Sweet'N Low was the answer. People admitted to hospitals for minor surgeries began stealing Sweet'N Low packets first from the food tray, then from the supply closet. Once released, they called Cumberland to ask if they could buy the product in bulk. By the early 1960s, pink packets could be found on every table in every diner on the East Coast. By the mid-1960s, boxes of Sweet'N Low were stocked in the baking aisle of supermarkets all around the country, as if it were a staple. Market success depends on identifying a personal desire that's broadly shared. If it's true for me, it'll be true for millions. In waging a struggle with his weight, Ben had satisfied a general need. In satisfying a general need, he'd plugged into the zeitgeist and boarded the money train.

But fortunes are double-edged: there is the useful and

good; there is the destructive and bad. Useful because money makes everything easier. Destructive because money turns people into jerks. The story of the Eisenstadts is the story of what happens to a typically dysfunctional middle-class American family when a hundred million dollars rains down. Ben became angry, Betty stingy, demanding, and mean, Marvin haughty and unreachable. Ira came to believe it was okay to spend your life in a mansion with a hundred cats. Ellen became insecure, paranoid. And Gladys, who'd been mildly disturbed, went completely insane. She'd had psoriasis since she was a teenager, an autoimmune disorder that turned her skin blotchy and red; psoriasis patches look like scales. According to the Mayo Clinic, 250 million people have been diagnosed with the condition—that is, 2 to 3 percent of the world's population. It's highly treatable. Cortisone. Vitamin D. Sunshine. Diet. Exercise. But, with all that money enabling her, Gladys refused to see a doctor, then fixed on the disease to explain her unhappiness. Urged to get outside into the heat and watch her diet, Gladys instead retreated to a dark chilled room on the ground floor of her parents' house, where she watched TV, talked on the phone, and ordered pizza and Chinese food, with a preference for Hung Chao's signature dish, Fatty Duck. "The worst goddamn thing for her," Herbie said, "and she ordered it five, six times a week."

Ben urged Gladys to get out, get a job, live her life, but the more he urged, the more stubborn she became. She screamed, insulted, threw dishes, and pounded the wall, yelling, "Look at me! Look at me! Look at me! I hate you! I hate you! I hate you!" Untreated, her ordinary case of psoriasis deteriorated into arthritic psoriasis. Her fingers cramped with pain. Finally, a doctor was called. He examined her in the room, then gave her a choice: she could get out of bed, seek treatment, and begin physical therapy or have her fingers surgically fused to relieve the pain. Without Ben's money, she would have been forced to get up, get out, get going. With it, she was able to afford the surgery, which is why her hands worked less like gloves than like mittens. With minor exceptions, Gladys spent the next forty years in bed.

No. 20

HERBIE AND ELLEN HAD DINNER IN MIDWOOD EVERY FRIDAY night. This was not a request but a requirement that Betty called a tradition. It must have been connected to the Jewish Sabbath, but any hint of religion had washed away. Only a few inscrutable rituals remained. There was no God, but there were candles. There were no prayers, but there was music. They were like Spanish conversos, practicing customs that lost their meaning long ago.

Herbie hated the dinners. They were boring and awkward, and it got worse after he made the mistake of asking Ben if he could borrow a few thousand dollars for a down payment on a house. Ben, who was then selling more than a hundred million packets of Sweet'N Low a year, said that though he'd like to help, his assets were tied up in long-term investments and he "wasn't liquid."

Also, the waiting. Herbie spent at least an hour alone every Friday night killing time until Marvin and his wife, Barbara, arrived. He was left by himself in the living room while Betty took Ellen upstairs to show off her newest rings and brooches and the children went back to the cold dark room to be propagandized by Gladys.

One night, he'd had enough. After thirty minutes in the living room, he went into the kitchen and crawled under the table, where he was hidden by a long tablecloth. "Let them wait for *me*," he said to himself. "Let's see how they like it." He stayed there for ten, twenty, thirty minutes. He stayed until he heard Ellen wandering the house, calling his name. She looked in the living room, the dining room, the kitchen. She asked the maid—her name was Edith and she had eleven fingers, with a second pinkie on her left hand that did nothing—then went to look for him outside. Just as Herbie was about to crawl out, two pairs of feet appeared beneath the tablecloth, sensible loafers on this side, glittery pumps on that. Ben and Betty! Ben admonished Betty in dulcet tones. He'd gotten a bill from Edna Nelkin's jewelry store on Nostrand Avenue. Betty had spent forty thousand dollars at the store in June. "I'm not saying you can't get what you want," Ben told Betty. "I'm just asking you to be more discerning."

Herbie waited under the table long after Ben and Betty had gone. When he finally clambered out, it was into a new world, with a different state of mind. He could hardly look at Ben after that. The Friday night dinners, which had merely been pointless and boring, became excruciating. He began inventing reasons to skip: he said he had to work late on a project, or was coming down with a fever or a sprue. Or he simply didn't show.

When Ellen called the house, he'd pick up as if there were nothing amiss.

"Hello."

"Where the hell are you?"

"What do you mean? Where the hell are *you*?"

"At my parents' house!"

Pause.

"Wait. What day is this?"

When offered a promotion that would mean relocating to Illinois, he gripped the opportunity with both hands. There were risks and unknowns, but one thing was certain: he'd never have to go to another Friday night dinner.

No. 21

HERBIE HAD ASCENDED FROM ALLSTATE TO ITS PARENT company, Sears, where he was named to the executive committee. At thirty-two years old, he was the youngest member of senior management, in charge of deal making and training, tasked with representing the company in meetings and teaching the other executives how to negotiate.

Sears began as a mail-order watch company in 1886, grew into a general catalog business, then was built into a behemoth by Julius Rosenwald, a German Jew from Springfield, Illinois. But Rosenwald died in 1932. By the time Herbie arrived thirty years later, the upper ranks had been taken over by Waspy Ivy League business school graduates. Arriving each morning, Herbie would sing out, "Company Jew, passing through!"

Given three weeks to relocate, he flew to Illinois, visited the office—a mirrored glass box beside the Edens Expressway in Lincolnshire, a suburb of Chicago—toured Libertyville, a town where many Sears executives lived, visited a few houses, purchased a split-level colonial in a neighborhood recently pried from a forest, then flew home.

The street was treeless, as exposed to the elements as the Sahara. The Des Plaines River, high and fast in March, sleepy and low in July, thick with ice in February, was a hundred yards from the front door.

Ellen was less than thrilled with the town. She was a Brooklyn girl, a product of subways, diners, Broadway shows. She'd never learned to drive. And here she was, frozen in the snowy semirural sticks.

"At least there are Jews," she said.

"How do you know that?" Herbie asked, surprised.

"There's a Chinese restaurant," she said.

As it turned out, Libertyville was maybe the only American town with Chinese food and no Jews. When asked if he encountered anti-Semitism in Libertyville, Herbie said, "Nah, they were happy we moved in. A neighbor said, 'Thank God. We were afraid they'd sell to Catholics.'"

Thus was born Herbie's new identity. He'd been a knock-around Brooklyn guy in Brooklyn, a grizzly in the North Woods. He'd now become a grizzly in town, a fish out of water, a Bensonhurst boy in the provinces. In such a circumstance, most people try to blend in. Herbie went the other way. ("When they zig, I zag," he'd explain.) He exaggerated his differences, played up and accentuated the Brooklyn parts of his identity. His accent became thicker in Libertyville, his voice louder. He wore sweat suits and his Lafayette letterman's jacket on the weekends. He greeted strangers in town, stood in line with the cars at the bank drive-through—a human among machines—shouted across the street to friends the way he'd shouted to Inky, Bucko, and Who Ha. People loved him in Libertyville, and he loved them right back. He was a character, a small-town celebrity, the sort of oddball you went to with a problem. He helped neighbors work out their purchases and closings. His art of the deal was never about tricking an opponent. It was about making the other person feel respected, getting a good deal while letting the other guy feel he'd done the same. Win-win. "And it isn't because I want to be a good person," he'd explain. "It's because I want to be *effective*. If the other guy walks away feeling bad about what happened, the deal is going to fall apart and you're going to end up with nothing."

People often asked where he came from.

"Me?" he'd say in his Brooklynese. "I come from Cheyenne, Wyoming."

If asked what he did for a living in Cheyenne, he'd say, "I'm a Presbyterian minister."

He took to wearing a suede cowboy hat in Libertyville. It became a trademark. He said it identified his true character. He might talk like a Dead End Kid, but he was really a cowboy, a High Plains drifter. "I fix a problem, settle a feud, bring peace to the people, then move on."

A woman in town became obsessed with him and insisted on painting his picture, which hung in the window of the Libertyville art shop for years.

Being the only New Yorker in town, the only street corner guy, did not bother Herbie. In fact, he loved it. It gave him a new shtick—the comedy of contrast.

No. **22**

HIS OLDEST CHILD, SHARON, WAS SEVEN WHEN THE FAMily moved to Illinois. Herbie and Ellen being the only Jewish parents in town made Sharon the only Jewish kid in school. Mostly it was nothing you'd notice, but not always. If a kid did something stupid, another kid would say, "Don't be such a Polack." If a kid did something weak, another kid would say, "Don't be such a girl." If a kid did something cheap, another kid would say, "Don't be such a Jew."

No one likes to be turned into an adjective, especially when they're the sole example of the type. This was a childhood far from that experienced by Herbie or Ellen, so there was not much Herbie could say other than "Ignore it." As for Ellen, she ascribed it, as she ascribed all acts of indecency directed at her children, to jealousy. "They're pea green with envy," she'd say.

Ellen took Sharon aside the summer before fourth grade and said, "I've got good news."

"What is it, Ma?"

"There'll be another Jewish kid in school next year."

"Who is it, Ma?"

"Your brother Steven."

Cut to Steven: a tough five-year-old, six-year-old, seven-, eight-, nine-, ten-year-old. His eyes, deep and oddly intense for a kid—one blue, the other green—gave him the look of a grade-school intimidator. It's a quality he's never lost: you don't mess with him for fear of what he'll do. He was never a cool kid but was never anything other than cool; he was a force apart, surrounded by a small group of worshipful contemporaries who figured he'd always have a plan, an answer, a way out. In other words, he was a lot like Herbie.

Ellen hoped Sharon would look out for Steven in school, but Ellen had it backward. It was not Steven who'd need protection, but the opposite. He'd become a playground big shot by fourth grade, the go-to guy behind the swings, the sort of junkyard fighter Tom Hagen has in mind in *The Godfather* when he says, "Even Sonny won't be able to call off Luca Brasi."

This put him at cross-purposes with Sharon, who, having started as a junior school patrol officer in third grade, climbed the ranks to a senior bus monitor, charged with keeping peace on the very route that Steven kept in turmoil from 3:05 to 3:22 each afternoon.

Sharon, who walked the aisle of the bus in a red sash, warned Steven several times in the fall of 1973. When he carried on, she issued him first an unofficial warning, then an official warning, then a second notice, and finally a pink slip. He was to appear at a meeting with the principal, vice-principal, bus driver, and senior bus monitor. In the meantime, he was banned from the bus. When Herbie and Ellen found out, they were angrier at Sharon than at Steven. For Ellen, it meant she'd have to drive Steven to school each morning and home each afternoon, wait in that line, deal with the snowy roads and her fear behind the wheel. For Herbie, it meant Sharon had failed to understand an essential part of an ancient code. If you have a problem with your brother, you deal with it *inside* the family. Don't rat; don't turn your brother in to the cops.

It was another one of his big lessons. Loyalty. Without that, you have nothing. A fan of Westerns, he used to quote Sam Peckinpah's *The Wild Bunch*, tugging at his hat and saying, "When you side with a man, you stay with him, and if you can't do that, you're like some animal. You're finished. We're finished. All of us."

No. 23

I WAS BORN THE DAY NEIL ARMSTRONG TOOK HIS FIRST "small step" onto the moon—minus a year, plus ten days. July 30, 1968. I'm the only member of the family born in the Midwest. Lake Forest Hospital, where the nurses poured champagne in every room, even delivery. My mother once told me I was "an accident," quickly adding, "a wonderful accident."

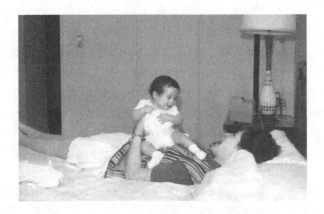

Herbie and Ellen had a perfect family. One girl, one boy—environmentally responsible, replacement numbers. They thought their work in child creation was done in 1963. I arrived like a party crasher ringing the bell at 4:00 a.m., shouting, "I know someone's in there."

I was barely four pounds at birth, weak and sickly. My twisted legs took months to repair. Without modern medicine, I would have been like a cripple in Dickens. There was something wrong with my heart, too. "He's got a bum ticker," a doctor said. I had to be brought to the hospital every few weeks for an EKG. At some point, a doctor said, "He'll eventually need a heart transplant."

My mother went home after getting this news, got out the scissors, and cut off all her hair. As it sometimes turns out, the doctor, though correct in many specifics, missed the big picture. Without going into detail, it's enough to say that I am fifty-two years old as I write this and still in possession of my original heart.

My sister claims that I was treated better, more gingerly, with greater care, than she and Steven because my parents believed I would not be around very long. Though I can't prove it, I believe the way I was handled in those early years—my continued existence was accepted after age eight, when a new procedure revealed I'd been misdiagnosed—explains the perfect memory I have for faces, houses, rooms, and voices.

Close your eyes.

Think back.

What's the first thing you remember?

For me, it's a family gathering, a bris—the circumcision performed, as prescribed in the Bible, on the eighth day of a boy's life. (God in Genesis: "Every man child among you shall be circumcised. And ye shall circumcise the flesh of your foreskin and it shall be a token of the covenant betwixt you and me.")

Whose bris?

My own.

People tell me it's impossible, that I remember not what happened but what someone told me happened, or what I dreamed or imagined, but I know what I know. The ceremony was performed in the living room in Libertyville. I remember the carpet (burnt orange), the walls (red brick), the buffet (smoked fish, rugelach). I remember my bassinet and my blue outfit. I remember the gargoyle faces of my aunts and uncles. I remember the wine-soaked napkin that, shoved between my lips when the cutting was done, plunged me back into the void.

Then I'm three or four years old, standing in the driveway in front of the house, watching my brother and father play basketball. Herbie is in a wheelchair, having snapped his Achilles tendon while playing in a pickup game with men half his age. He dribbles with one hand while navigating the wheelchair with the other, like a guy in a movie about Vietnam vets. Then I'm in his office and he's blowing smoke into the aluminum tube that held the cigar and sealing it. Later, when I open the tube, the smoke drifts out, like a transmigration of souls. Then we are driving through a landscape I can't quite place. My father is playing a Frank Sinatra song on the eight track called "Noah," which includes the lyric "You've got to walk with the lion."

"What do you have to be to walk with a lion?" he asks.

"You have to be brave," my brother answers.

"Wrong," says my father, laughing. "You have to be a lion."

Some of these might not even be my memories. They might be stories that grew in my mind while looking through the box of pictures my mother kept in a kitchen drawer. My brother, my sister, and I walking in the barren woods in winter.

My father at the wheel of his Karmann Ghia, cigar in mouth, split-level colonials buried in snow. Laundry hung on

a cord in Mundelein, Illinois, that clean starchy smell. A circus tent. A Ferris wheel rotating at night.

Herbie led a nine-to-five existence at Sears. He was what his uncles would have called a "jobnik," up at six, heavy-lidded in rush hour, home by the other six, which, from October until March, meant he left in the dark and returned in the dark. His routine was more stable and traditional than it ever had been or ever would be again. He spent weekends around the house, leading us along the Des Plaines River in pursuit of adventure. We searched for the lost treasures of Billy the Kid and Father Marquette. We hunted grouse, snipe, Cornish game hen, turkey. He asked us to follow him onto the frozen Des Plaines River. Steven, having been warned by a teacher about black ice, refused. Herbie jumped on the ice to prove its stability, then fell through. I think of this whenever he quotes one of his favorite sayings: "If you're walking on thin ice, you might as well dance."

He told us stories at night. Whereas other kids heard about Hansel and Gretel, Pinocchio, or the Three Bears, we heard about Bucko, Who Ha, Inky, Zeke the Creek, Gutter Rat. Herbie was the hero of these stories. He got his friends into trouble, then got them out. There was no apparent point to his behavior, no reward. It was just about the challenge, the fun. He did it so he could talk about it later. He did it because what is life if not all the crap you did tallied and described? Of course, there was a point, though it was hidden. He'd been training himself for a career in negotiation, for life in the adult world, which was just the kid world amplified and for real.

No. 24

IT WAS ALL THE DRIVING THAT CONVINCED HERBIE AND Ellen of the need to move out of Libertyville. The precipitating event happened shortly before my fifth birthday. Because there was no prekindergarten in town, my mother or father or the housekeeper, named Bea, shuttled me to a school in Highland Park twice a week, a fifteen-mile trip each way.

While we were stopped at a red light one afternoon—I had just seen two trains speeding in opposite directions on parallel tracks, for me a premonition of disaster ever since—a car plowed into us from behind. I was in the passenger seat without a seat belt. Bea threw me back at the moment of impact, saving my life but sending her into the steering wheel. Turning to me, she said, "You're fine," and as she said this, blood poured from her mouth. I fainted. When I opened my eyes, a paramedic was pulling me from the car. My eyelashes were scattered across my shirt. They'd fallen out from shock. Herbie and Ellen began looking for a house closer to the city—closer to the airport, closer to shopping and schools— the next day.

Herbie quit his job. Sears had been lending him out to other companies, where, for a fee paid to the home office, he'd analyze their operations, negotiate their deals, train their workers. It had been only a matter of time until he decided to cut out the middleman and do this work on his own, selling his services directly. He'd never again work in a single location or office, but in towns and cities around the world. There was some thought of moving back to New York, but Chicago, with its big, centrally located airport—halfway between JFK and LAX—was the best place to headquarter such a peripatetic career.

Herbie and Ellen looked in half a dozen towns—Wilmette, Winnetka, Evanston—before settling on a split-level ranch in Highland Park. Houses, good houses, could be had for a song back then. America is an arrow. In the years that followed Watergate, it was pointing down. A ten-bedroom mansion could be purchased on Chicago's North Shore for five hundred thousand dollars. The Highland Park house listed at eighty thousand. Herbie agreed to pay sixty thousand dollars, fixtures and furniture included. While waiting for approval from the bank to schedule a closing, he left on a long work trip. Each day, after speaking to executives in office courts or hotel ballrooms in Wisconsin, Minnesota, or Iowa, he'd call Ellen from his motel room and ask, "What happened today?" always wanting and expecting the same answer, "Nothing."

Then, one day, instead of saying "Nothing," she said, "I bought a house."

He corrected her: "You mean that we're *buying* a house."

"No," she said. "I withdrew that offer and bought a different house. In Glencoe."

He corrected her again: "You mean you saw a house you like in Glencoe and want to withdraw the Highland Park offer."

"No," she said. "I mean I found a house I liked in Glencoe and bought it."

Herbie stared at the twenty-two-inch Magnavox across the room, saying nothing. February. Frost on the motel windows. Ellen could hear Johnny Carson doing his monologue: "Last night, it was so cold the flashers in New York were only describing themselves."

"Okay," said Herbie. "Start again at the beginning."

Ben and Betty—Ellen's parents—had flown from New York to help with the children. In the middle of the week, maddened by boredom, Ben told Ellen he wanted to see the new house. They met the realtor in Highland Park. Ben walked through the rooms, examining floorboards, looking out windows, muttering—he was a gruff, opinionated man— then asked the realtor if she had other properties for sale in the area. They followed her into Glencoe, where Ben fell in love with a creaky wreck of a house, a five-bedroom English Tudor that had been through nearly a century of hard weather and rowdy families. It was more than twice the price Herbie wanted to pay, a difference Ben promised to cover. Ben made a first offer that night, handled the negotiation, then closed at $120,000.

My mother took us to see the house the next day. It was at the end of a root-buckled street shaded by elm trees, many marked for destruction. This was year zero of the Dutch elm blight. The Highland Park house had been mid-century modern, close to new, sensible, well ordered, clean—America as it wanted to become. The Glencoe house was rambling, drafty, and old—America as it actually was. There were hidden staircases, false doors, dumbwaiters, laundry chutes, and a basement that flooded whenever it rained. The kitchen had been remodeled during the Eisenhower administration. Every appliance was state of the art circa 1953. Restaurant-grade keep-hot lights, built-in toaster, and built-in can opener, all of it broken. There were two chimneys, one for the fireplace, one for the incinerator, an industrial-size trash burner, use of which had been banned generations before. If you reached in,

---

you could pull out scraps of the newspaper saved by the reprieve: *Chicago Daily Tribune*, December 1935: "Gem Plot Exposed as Hoax"; "Britain Washes Hands of Peace Plan at Geneva."

We had picked our rooms before my father even learned of the purchase. When he tried to back out, my mother said, "We'll lose the deposit. And Richard's already made a friend." (That would be the kid across the street, Dennis.)

When Ellen called Ben in Brooklyn a few nights before the closing, he cursed under his breath, then said, "I forgot all about it." He told my mother he did not have the money to give her, that he'd planned to, only to realize, on his return to work, that his money was tied up in investments and he was "not liquid."

Herbie put in the money he'd been saving for renovations, then called *his* father, Morris, who, though he was, to borrow a phrase from Miami Beach, "living on a fixed income," wired the difference without comment. When Herbie promised to pay it back, Morris waved him off, saying, "It's a gift. Never mention it again."

And so the Cohens came to inhabit 1062 Bluff Road in Glencoe, Illinois, where the *s* is silent and the populace hardy. That house was the only place I have ever felt truly at home. It's where my mind goes when I feel sick, mistreated, sorry for myself, or lonely. I dream I'm back in that house, usually hiding from the new owners, at least once a month.

No. 25

A PERSON FROM GLENCOE WILL TELL ANOTHER PERSON, usually a person from the East, "I grew up on the beach, just like in that Dick Dale song," but my wife, Jessica, who is from Connecticut, told me I did not grow up on the beach because the beach means the ocean, which is thousands of miles either way from Illinois, but those of us who came of age on Chicago's North Shore know Lake Michigan for what it is—a mighty inland sea, subject to storms and tides, ringed by more than a thousand miles of beach. According to a map, Chicago is across the water from St. Joseph, Michigan, but if you'd asked the childhood me what was on the other side, I'd have told you, "Paris."

Glencoe is nineteen miles north of the city. Its expensive homes are built on the rim of a ravine that overlooks the lake, which, like the sky, changes color with time and season. It's a mood ring that reveals the temper of the town—black in winter, gray in autumn, green in spring, blue as the Mediterranean in summer. There are harbors and bays along the coast, mooring fields with fishing boats, sailboats, yachts. There are tiny private beaches and a sprawling public beach with a raft and a pier and a lifeguard. A stone path leads from the beach to Park Avenue, which you can follow into town.

We were free in that town in the summer in a way kids will never be free again. Our parents, having released us after breakfast, did not reclaim us until dinner, then released us again. We did not go home until we could see Venus. We roamed in hordes, like gangs, pedaled our bikes to the lake, pedaled our bikes to the forest preserve, pedaled our bikes to the lagoon where the mob dumped bodies. We hung around older kids, big brothers and cousins, listening to their stories about old Glencoe, the way it used to be. If it happened more than three years earlier, it was history. If it happened more than ten, it was Noah and the Flood. We heard about stores that existed before these stores, teachers before these teachers, slang before this slang. We heard about Big Ed Walsh and the Bird Man, Mike Bloomfield and Kenesaw Mountain Landis, about the day the woods caught fire, about the ghost that emerges from the lake on moonless nights.

There were two commercial streets in Glencoe, Vernon and Park. Within a hundred yards of that intersection, you could get anything a person would ever need for a good life—records (Wally King's), sporting goods (Ray's), customized T-shirts (You Name It), pizza (Little Red Hen), hot dogs (Big Al's), hardware (Wienecke's). When it came to essentials, there was two of everything—two delis, two pharmacies, two banks—which taught you all you'd ever need to know about market economics.

We had lunch at Ricky's Delicatessen our first day in town. Before we were finished, Herbie knew half the people in the place. He went out to the alley to smoke a cigar with Ricky himself. He was soon as well known in Glencoe as he had been in Libertyville. He had a way of turning every place into Brooklyn.

It was a depressing time in America, post-everything. Post-Vietnam. Post-Watergate. Three Mile Island, stagflation, Billy Beer, malaise—this was the afterpiece, the dregs, the silt bottom. Everything was broken. Everyone's parents were divorced. Everyone was on drugs or in recovery. Herbie built a bubble to protect us from all the negativity. There was no divorce in our house, nor talk of divorce—no video games, no drugs, no drug talk. My parents didn't even know the language. At most, my father might mention a "funny cigarette," or my mother, worried about my sister, might advise her to never "smell cocaine."

It was less like growing up in the 1980s than in the 1950s. When a consortium of towns asked Herbie to handle the negotiations meant to bring us cable TV, he violated his own rule, striking a deal so favorable it seemed punitive, causing the parent company to pull out. When asked about it—our township remained one of the few in America without cable for years—he'd insist he'd done it intentionally. He said it was his way of "giving the kids around here another decade of the old-fashioned childhood; they'll thank me when they're thirty."

He pranked and goofed on us constantly. In this way, he was expressing another part of his philosophy. Don't act as if you know what's going to happen; you don't. And: the sky is gray and the windchill brutal, but you can still have fun. Leaving a movie theater or restaurant, we'd race through the cold to the car, the station wagon or Cadillac. We'd be frantically tugging on the locked doors when he strolled up, cigar in mouth, whistling a Sinatra tune. He'd go to the driver's side, unlock the door, get in, fix the rearview mirror, then the side mirror, adjust his seat, fumble with the keys, start the engine, crank up the heat, readjust the vents, all the while ignoring our screams and hammering. He'd put the car in reverse, back up five feet, then suddenly seem to notice us. He'd slap his forehead, unlock the doors, and say, "I didn't even see you."

He refused to wear anything heavier than a windbreaker even when it was ten below, explaining, "It's because of my genetic heritage. Unlike you all, who take after your mother, I come from a hearty stock and was built for cold."

He was a man of tremendous appetites. For comedy, success, love, and food. He was one of those human yo-yos who can gain or drop a hundred pounds in a few months. Binge and fast. Consume and forsake. Sin and repent. Enjoy and suffer. This was good for his tailor but bad for his blood pressure, blood sugar, knees, and back. I worried about his health constantly. All the needles touched red, but he just went on smoking, bingeing, running, fasting. He read the newspaper while he drove! When trying to scare him straight, I asked, "What will I do if you die?" He did not answer as most fathers would—"You will be fine"—but focused on my second clause, saying, "Nothing can kill me. I will never die."

He was the worst kind of helicopter parent with my sister. He says the key to success is caring, but not *that* much, but when it came to his oldest child, he cared too much. He pushed her into clubs, bigfooted her school assignments. She hated sports, but he sent her onto the court or field anyway. He believed the experience would teach her about teamwork and competition, how to handle victory, how to suffer defeat. When she rejected softball, he signed her up for basketball. When she gave up on that, he sent her to horseback-riding camp, where, bucked by a horse named Grandma, she broke her wrist. He'd ride behind her in the car as she trained for track, cigar in mouth, blasting the horn when she slowed, shouting, "Move it!"

The college application process—that was the worst. He wanted her to have the college experience he'd missed, which meant a small school with a nice campus. Amherst. Williams. My sister was accepted by Carleton, a liberal arts school in Minnesota that fit the bill, but she decided to go to Tulane in New Orleans instead, partly because of the weather, partly because of the locale, partly because she knew it would drive him nuts. When people asked where Sharon was going to college, Herbie would say, "She was accepted by Carleton."

He was tough on my brother, too. When he heard Steven was being tormented by bullies at school, Herbie drove him to the ringleader's house and made him knock on the door and ask the kid to come outside and fight, the presumption being that bullies are cowards who operate only in packs. (He was right about that.) He pushed him to play ice hockey because "hockey will make you tough." He insisted on Brooklyn Rules when playing basketball in the driveway, which he explained this way: "If you go over me for a layup, you're gonna pay a price."

He gave my brother the same list of colleges he'd given my sister. When my brother rejected these, Herbie, having softened with age, said, "Fine. Go anywhere you can get in, with one exception: NYU. I want you at a college with a campus."

So that's where Steven went: NYU.

Having failed to impose his will on my siblings, Herbie let me skate. "Kids are like pancakes," he'd say. "You should be allowed to throw out the first batch. There's nothing wrong with the batter; the grill wasn't hot enough." He'd wised up when my turn came. And just wasn't around that much, leaving him little time to mold me. Having experienced a first flush of big success, he'd become fixated on his career. He was giving as many as 250 speeches a year when I was in middle school, traveling from boardroom to boardroom, from convention to convention, and leading negotiations around the world. He'd begun to write columns for the local papers and to appear as an expert on Chicago TV. His funny stories and sayings always seemed to have a message, though it could be inscrutable: "A nose that can hear is worth two that can smell." "Why ask the monkey, when you can ask the organ grinder?"

He wore two watches, one on each wrist.

"A man with one watch thinks he knows the time," he'd explain, "but a man with two watches knows he can never be sure."

He became the subject of magazine articles. His speaking fee doubled, doubled again. He landed a regular gig on Chicago's ABC TV affiliate, WLS, where, twice a week, he shared his thoughts on everything from Mayor Daley to Super Rats.

Over time, without meaning or wanting to, he gathered a group of disciples. He became a kind of guru. People called at all hours looking for answers: *Should I forgive my husband? What should I do with my business? How should I live my life?* A woman named Gretchen Ole—she'd been to several of his lectures—phoned whenever something troubled her in the news. *There's a leak at Three Mile Island?* Call Herbie. *Reagan wants to build a missile command system to blast Russian nukes out of the sky?* Call Herbie. It infuriated my mother, who wanted an unlisted number. Herbie wouldn't hear of it; if you got him on the phone, he was going to talk as long as you wanted. His attitude was this: if you need me, I'll help. It was my father's strength and his weakness. He did not want to cut off the disciples, because they made him feel needed.

People went to him for many reasons. He taught them tricks, strategies that could help them navigate life. He taught them how to buy a house, sell a car, end a partnership. Some of his advice was counterintuitive. If you really want a house, you can't speed the process by offering the asking price, because the seller will think he has set the price too low and back out. If you want to end a war, quit while your opponent is still confident and strong. You must leave him with self-respect if you don't want an enemy for life.

At the core, all his lessons were about the same thing: empowerment. He tried to wake people up to the power they had without knowing it. He especially loved advising the underdog, the self-defeated who has been crushed by the institution, the machine. "You're never out of options," he'd say. "There's always something to be done."

His philosophy had been informed by his reading of history, his life in Brooklyn, and the impression made by certain works of art. His favorite passage came from Viktor Frankl's book *Man's Search for Meaning*, where the last human freedom is defined as the freedom "to choose one's attitude in any given set of circumstances, to choose one's own way.

"And there were always choices to make," Frankl goes on. "Every day, every hour, offered the opportunity to make a decision, a decision which determined whether you would or would not submit to those powers which threatened to rob you of your very self, your inner freedom."

Herbie believed he could talk his way into every kind of office, room, situation. It was all about confidence, he'd say, behaving as if you belonged. Larry told me about the night Herbie bluffed his way into the Democratic National Convention. Madison Square Garden 1992. Larry and Herbie had dinner; then, as he went off to host his show from the convention floor, Larry said, "I wish I could take you with me, Herbie, but the security is insane."

Herbie: "I'll meet you on the stage."

Larry: "No way."

"And the next thing I know, I'm standing there, talking to Al Gore, and here comes Herbie, walking out onto the stage."

I figured he'd slipped someone a fifty, or something, but Herbie scoffed at the suggestion. "It's not money that gets you in," he told me. "It's authority. Power."

According to a reporter friend who'd been there, Herbie had walked up to the head of security and started asking questions about crowd size and deployment. The guard answered each question carefully, in great detail. Then Herbie slapped him on the back, thanked him for his service, and went inside.

When I was in college in New Orleans, he wanted to have dinner at Commander's Palace, the best restaurant in town. I told him the place was sold out for months, that we'd "never get in." He insisted we go anyway. He walked to the desk and said, "Herb Cohen, table for three."

"Do you have a reservation?"

"No."

"We're completely booked."

Herbie threw up his hands, turned to my mother, and said, "I guess Ella was wrong."

"Ella?" said the maître d', confused.

"Ella Brennan, a friend of mine. She said I should just come over and you'd seat us. No worries."

Five minutes later we were at a table for four in the corner.

"Who is Ella Brennan?" I asked.

"She owns this place," said Herbie.

"Do you really know her?"

"Of course he doesn't," said my mother. "There was a story about her in the in-flight magazine."

We walked by the Museum of Modern Art in New York on my wedding day. I wanted to go in and see a particular painting, but the line went around the corner.

"You don't have to wait in that line," said Herbie.

"Of course you do," I said.

"Well, maybe you do," he said. "Not me."

We bet ten dollars. Five minutes later, we were standing in front of the painting on the third floor. He'd gone in the employee entrance in back, where he told the man behind the desk that we'd come from the Governor's Commission for the Police Athletic League and needed to examine a painting on the third floor.

Bingo.

Some of his tricks were practical. "If you don't remember a person's name," he told me, "ask them if they still live in the same place. Don't ask them about their children, because maybe they have no children. And don't ask them about their spouse, because maybe that person died. But if you ask them if they still live in the same place, then either they *are* still living in the same place and are amazed that you remember, or they've have moved and think it considerate of you to inquire."

It was less advice disciples got from him than a sense of security. That's what Larry got, too—the sense that no matter how badly he messed up, Herbie could save him. Larry was constantly in trouble when I was a kid. Herbie was constantly getting him out of it, or trying to. At one point, Larry was being extorted by a woman. I don't remember all the details, but it had to do with pictures and a demand for money. Herbie told Larry they needed to go to the FBI.

"Why?" asked Larry.

"Why? Because this person is committing a crime!"

The FBI arranged a sting. Larry's bagman would meet the woman on the train platform at Union Station in Washington, D.C., where he'd hand over the cash and get the photos. As soon as the exchange was complete, the FBI would swoop in to make the arrest. Everyone agreed: Herbie would be the bagman. He loved this kind of stuff. The subterfuge, the cloak-and-dagger—it's how every kid imagines adulthood will be. Told to dress inconspicuously, he turned up in his Lafayette letterman's jacket and cowboy hat, then was wired for sound. The extortionist had meanwhile tipped the *National Enquirer*, which had sent a reporter and a photographer. The resulting three-page spread—Herbie looking over his shoulder as he hands over the money, taking the photos, then giggling as he walks way—was denounced as a shanda by my grandma Esther, a careful reader of the supermarket tabloids, but Herbie loved it.

Over time, he became less of a business guru than a comedian and a philosopher. He was *for* something—win-win negotiation. And he was also *against* something—life as a zero-sum game, meaning if you win, I lose. Herbie wouldn't want to live that way even if it were true, but it wasn't. He came to believe just the opposite: our fates are intertwined; the only way for me to win is for you to win, too.

No. **26**

IN THE LATE 1970S, MY PARENTS STARTED A BUSINESS
called Power Negotiations. Ellen designed the logo: two men
shaking hands, each with his thumb up. Win-win. This company sold a single product and derived its revenue from a
single source: Herbie. Seminars, keynotes, negotiations. He
described his mediation fee as "a minuscule percentage of an
astronomical sum." He did not like to speak at colleges, he
said, because colleges gave an honorarium, which means
"more honor, less arium."

Ellen booked the jobs and the travel from a suite in the
Ron of Japan building, an office that overlooked the Edens
Expressway and the botanical gardens. The business grew by
word of mouth. Herbie was soon putting on seminars for the
FBI in Quantico, Virginia, where he taught conflict resolu-
tion and terrorist negotiation. He went on to lecture agents
and advise leadership at the Departments of State, Justice,
and the Treasury, as well as at the CIA. He helped design the
FBI's Behavioral Science Unit, famed for the elaborate personality profiles it uses to catch serial killers. In explaining the
point of this work, he'd quote Arthur Miller's play *The Price*:
"You can't know the price, if you don't know the player." This
had been his position since the Moppo days: to reach a deal,
you have to know what the other side needs, and to know
that, you have to know who the other side is.

In 1980, he was brought to the White House to advise
Jimmy Carter during the Iran hostage crisis. After meeting
with the president and his counselors, Herbie went on TV
and predicted the day and time the hostages would be

released. He was off by just seven minutes. As much as anything, the accuracy of this prediction made his name. When
asked how he'd done it, he explained his reasoning in terms
that might be considered offensive today, which doesn't make
them less true.

For the Iranians, the hostages were like fifty-two Persian
rugs put on a wall for sale. And here comes the American
Jimmy Carter; what's the first thing he says when he gets into
the bazaar? "I'm not leaving here without those rugs." What
just happened to the price? The Iranians made mistakes, too. If
they wanted top dollar, they needed to close before the November election, their moment of maximum leverage. They
missed it, and the price collapsed, at which point Herbie looked
for the next deadline. When was it? January 20, 1981, Ronald
Reagan's inauguration day. The Iranians had been dealing with
a peaceful Georgian who'd repeatedly said he had to have those
rugs, but who's coming up the road? Cowboy Dutch twirling
his pistols and saying he might just blow up the market instead.
"Once you had all that figured out, making the prediction was
easy," Herbie said later. "When will the hostages be released?
Three minutes before Ronald Reagan takes office."

Herbie met with President-elect Reagan and suggested he
make a tough statement on Iran to drive the hostage takers to
deal with Carter. On December 28, 1980, when asked about
the terms he might offer, Reagan said, "I don't think you pay
ransom for people that have been kidnapped by barbarians."

Herbie went on to advise several presidents, including Bill
Clinton and the first George Bush, who put him on the team
that negotiated nuclear arms reduction with Russia, later
known as START.

As his fame grew, so did the oddness and variety of the tasks he was asked to perform. The dramatist David Mamet sent Herbie a draft of *Glengarry Glen Ross*, his play about real estate salesmen, for a verisimilitude read. *Does it ring true?* Herbie loved the play and suggested a single change—second prize for the contest at the end should be a set of new steak knives, a change that made it into the play and has become a staple of the Mamet canon. *The steak knives, those goddamn steak knives.* "Because that's what you got if you won the claims adjuster race at Allstate in the 1960s," Herbie explained. "First prize: steak knives. Second: you don't get fired."

But speeches and seminars remained the heart of his business. He ran one- and two-day sessions for businesses all over America, then all over the world. No matter the audience, his message was the same: stay detached, don't become fixated on a particular outcome, care, but not *that* much. (Jimmy Carter cared too much.) If you approach a negotiation as if it were a game, you'll have more fun and be more successful. If you approach life as if it were a negotiation, you'll care less, achieve more, and live longer.

He who laughs lasts.

There was a lot of setup necessary for a seminar. Packets had to be copied, collated, and handed out, notebooks and stacks of cash distributed; the latter were used in mock negotiations. My sister traveled with Herbie and worked for him on some of these trips. She complained that he made her carry his bags. Then it was Steven's turn. Then it was mine.

We'd fly from O'Hare to a flyspeck regional airport, then make our way via rental car across the Midwest, traveling from downtown building to suburban office park. Like a rock band on tour, he'd deliver the same show with slight variation—"Hello, Cleveland!"—in each city. His style was less management guru than borscht belt comic, strategy cut with laughter, the elixir hidden in a chocolate egg cream.

I set up chairs and welcomed attendees, then stood off to the side as he wrote on a big flip board.

We were up each morning before six. He'd yawn when he woke, hair wild, knees stiff. His feet hit the floor like hammers. He'd shave in the bathroom with the door open so he could hear the TV. He'd practice new material as we sat at the buffet, then continue as we drove to the next town. He wanted to surprise audiences, to wrong-foot the yokels as in basketball; they think you're going this way, overcommit; then—*whoosh!*—you're gone. "Buy a man a fish, you feed him for a night. Teach a man to fish, he'll be dead in a year from mercury poisoning."

I got to know his routines by heart. Not a dud in the bunch, though of course I had my favorites. Like his story about "history's first negotiation," which he says is chronicled in the Bible. "God wanted to wipe out the original twin cities, those desert meccas of sin, Sodom and Gomorrah. Abraham was opposed, but how do you negotiate with the Almighty?

Talk about power differential! So what did Abraham do? Did he say, 'God, what is wrong with you? You're making a stupid mistake.' Of course not. He went with a humble, low-key approach. He said, 'Hi, God. It's me, Abraham. I was just thinking over your decision to destroy Sodom and Gomorrah. Another good decision, God, right as usual. But then a thought popped into my head. What if I could come up with fifty good men amid all the evil people there? Do you think it'd be okay to kill fifty good men along with the wicked?'

"For sure God will at least respond to Abraham," Herbie said. "How do we know that? Because you always get a response once you realize that no response is also a response. God said, 'Okay, Abraham. Find me fifty good men and I'll spare those cities.'

"Now Abraham has God at the table talking. That's most of the battle. From there, it's just about setting the price.

"'I hadn't really done a count,' Abraham adds. 'What if I'm five good people short?'

"'Okay, Abraham. Find me forty-five good men in Sodom and Gomorrah. That'll be enough.'

"'You know, God, I was speaking figuratively. I was really just making a point. For all I know, there may only be twenty-five good men in Sodom and Gomorrah.'

"'Okay,' said God. 'Find me twenty-five and we have a deal.'

"Abraham got God all the way down to ten, which Abraham couldn't in fact find, but that's beside the point. The point is this: Abraham got a great price! And how did he do it? By using his weakness, by appealing to God's strength.

"By ceding power, you gain power," he'd explain. "What are the most powerful words in a negotiation? Are they 'I'm

105

an expert. I know better?' No. They're 'Who?' 'Huh?' and
'Wha?' When it comes to negotiating, you'd be better off acting like you know less, not more. In some cases, dumb is smarter
than smart, and inarticulate is better than articulate. You want
to train yourself to say, 'I don't know' . . . 'You lost me' . . . 'Could
you repeat that?' The most powerful words in business are 'I
don't understand. Help me.' Divest yourself of preconceived no-
tions, biases, prejudices. Ignorance, even if feigned, will produce
curiosity, humility, open-mindedness, and the kind of innova-
tive ideas that may bring people together."

Being weak does not mean being powerless; that was his
point. He'd tell audiences about a prisoner in solitary confine-
ment who wants a cigarette. He asks the guard, and the guard,
under the impression the prisoner is powerless, laughs and
turns away. "But the situation looks different to the prisoner,"
Herbie said. "He knows there is always another option if
you're willing to take risks. He asks again, now in a booming
voice: 'Can I please have a cigarette?' This time, when the
guard turns away, the prisoner says, 'If I don't get it, I'm going
to bang my head against the wall until I'm bloody. When they
ask who did it, I'm naming you. They won't believe me, but
think of all the hearings you'll have to attend and all the reports you'll have to fill out, as opposed to giving me one
crummy cigarette.'"

Herbie's method was as old as Aesop: he told stories, and
each story had a moral. He taught tricks, too, methods to in-
crease effectiveness. There was, for example, the Nibble: You
go into a store, Brooks Brothers at Water Tower Place, say,
pick a salesman, and make him show you everything on the
rack. Then, just when he's about to lose patience, you tell him

that you're ready to buy. After you've been fitted for a suit and are walking to the register, you say, 'What kind of ties will you be throwing in with this?'"

He talked about the art of purchasing big-box items, like refrigerators. Trick one: ask when it goes on sale. Everything is always just about to go on sale. You'll always get that price. Trick two: ask, "What if?" "What if I buy four refrigerators?" Trick three: point out a blemish on the floor model and ask for a blemish discount. If there is no blemish, create one.

A master of telephone negotiation, he explained what to do when everything goes wrong on a call. "I'd never recommend hanging up on another person," he said. "That would be socially unacceptable. Hang up while *you're* talking. How can you convincingly hang up on yourself? Simple. Say the equivalent of 'Hey, I'm really glad you called. You know, I was just thinking about you yester—'" Click.

On the second day of a two-day seminar, he'd screen the movie *12 Angry Men*, because "*12 Angry Men* dramatizes every type of negotiation." In the course of the movie, which is set in the deliberation room during a murder trial, nearly the entire jury is moved, at the instigation of a character played by Henry Fonda, from convict to acquit. Herbie broke down each scene, freezing the action at crucial moments to explain how the need of each juror is determined and met.

I sat through this lecture on many occasions, and though it came to bore me, I loved the way he closed the talk, was thrilled, no matter how many times I heard it. Henry Fonda is walking down the courthouse steps into the rain-soaked city at the end of the day. Another juror, seeing him, calls out, "Hey, what's your name?"

"Davis," says Fonda.

The men shake hands, smile at each other, then part.

"And that's the big point, the message of this movie," Herbie said. "The most important people in your life, the people who have an impact and change everything, and you don't even know their names."

I loved it because, one, it struck me as profound and, two, that's my old man in a nutshell. To him, every good song, movie, or book is never about what it's about, which might be a deathly ill baseball player, or a shut-in with a prized collection of figurines, or a salesman who's gone off his rocker. It's about life. If it's beautiful, if it moves him, it's about life. But that's not how he phrased it. Here's how he phrased it: "It's not about a ballpark, you schmuck, it's about everything."

Here I speak specifically of his reaction to Frank Sinatra's version of the Joe Raposo song "There Used to Be a Ballpark." Every time we listened to it in the car, he'd tell me that Sinatra had improvised the last phrase—"the summer went so quickly this year"—which he considered the most important line in the song, "because it's not just the summer that goes so quickly; it's life."

He spent at least three hundred days on the road most years. We used to flip through his calendar and laugh. If you can name a company, he probably lectured there: IBM, Sony, Atari, Apple, GM, Ford, Hilton, Hyatt, DuPont, Sikorsky, Honeywell, Microsoft, Google. The list goes on and on. Many clients sent thank-you gifts after a seminar. That's how we got our bench press, our propane grill, our cotton candy machine. Sony sent promotional copies of every record they had in the pipeline; that's how I first heard the Clash.

The CEO of a company that dealt in antique cars asked Ellen if Herbie had any hobbies. Ellen, unable to think of anything other than cigars, said, "He likes to exercise."

When the treadmill arrived two weeks later, Herbie was appalled.

"What was I supposed to say?" asked Ellen.

"Oh, I don't know," said Herbie. "How about antique cars?"

No. **27**

A REPORTER CALLED THE OFFICE IN EARLY 1980. HE'D been assigned to profile Herbie for *Playboy*, one of the biggest magazines in America. The writer, a smart, young Ivy Leaguer named Andrew Tobias, spent a week following Herbie around—from lecture to office, office to house, house to delicatessen. Watching Tobias work—he talked to us at lunch, hung out as we played basketball, flew with Herbie to D.C.—is what made me want to be a writer, and not just any kind of writer, but a "freelance." It had the ring of freedom. "Freelance writer" took a place in my pantheon beside "stunt coordinator," "escape artist," and "daredevil."

Herbie was lucky. They could have assigned a hack to tell his story. He got Andrew Tobias instead, a good writer in the golden age of magazines, the age of Hunter Thompson, Tom Wolfe, and the New Journalism, which allowed for tremendous creativity. Tobias constructed the piece in that spirit, not in a standard journalistic voice, or even his own voice, but in Herbie's Brooklyn patois. Rather than follow the conventional formula, which would have meant opening with a clever lead ("Herb Cohen means business"; "Herb Cohen wants to make a deal") proceeding to a nut graph ("in the last decade, Herb Cohen has become one of the world's most famous negotiators") followed by a stage-setting description ("Herb Cohen, who lives on Chicago's North Shore with his wife and children, is lighting a cigar, his cavernous features cast in a flickering orange glow") leading to a section-ending promise ("Herb Cohen can teach you how to be more effective"), Tobias built his piece around Herbie's personality—not an academic expert, but a Damon Runyon character, a street corner raconteur, a Warrior and a Weasel driver from Bad K, a coach who can't stay on the sidelines. It was less conventional reportage than mind-meld method writing. Tobias did not depict Herbie. He became Herbie and then, as Herbie, wrote the story.

Each section was named for one of Herbie's strategies or observations. "The New House," "The Nibble." Herbie had wanted to write a book but could never figure out how to turn his talk into prose. As anyone who's transcribed a joke can tell you, crucial elements are lost in the process. Intonation, body language, emphasis. What had been living in person is often dead on the page. To work, it's got to be less about copying than about translating. Which is an art. That's what Herbie learned from Andrew Tobias.

Herbie's reverence for the written word had itself been an obstacle. He regarded a book as something holy. "When God wanted to tell his story," he'd say, "it's not a movie he made." Tobias brought the process down to earth, showed Herbie that his voice could in fact be a literary voice. And the structure! It was not a grand scholarly thesis that organized the piece; it was the stories and the voice. The big picture emerged from the little stories in the way of a Chuck Close painting. Up close, it looks like a plethora of discrete images, but when you step back, you see that those images come together to form a single picture.

No. 28

ANDREW TOBIAS REMAINED PART OF OUR LIVES EVEN AFter the story was published. My father admired him and, at some point, amid this admiration, fixed on the idea of setting him up on a date with my sister. Andrew resisted and Sharon resisted, but in the end they realized the only way out was through.

We were spending a week with friends at a house in Arlington, Virginia. The street was beautiful, long, and leafy. Andrew arrived at seven on a summer evening. He was dressed like a Senate page, blue blazer, white shirt, penny loafers, khakis, brown hair swept to the side. He must have been in his mid-twenties, a freelance writer and young politico, a future treasurer of the Democratic National Committee. He held the passenger-side car door open for Sharon; she leaned across and opened his door. We watched them drive away, then stood under a big elm tree as it got dark.

My father stayed up until Sharon returned.

"How did it go?" he asked, when she came in.

"Fine."

"Do you think you'll go on a second date?"

"Probably not."

"Why?"

"He's gay."

Andrew Tobias, as we later found out, was not just a gay man but the pseudonymous author of the groundbreaking memoir *The Best Little Boy in the World*.

My father stared at my sister for a long time, then said, "I have no idea what you're talking about."

No. 29

THE PROFILE RAN IN THE JUNE 1980 ISSUE OF *PLAYBOY*. Dorothy Stratten was on the cover as "Playmate of the Year." The issue would become a collector's item, made valuable by the murder of Stratten, killed that August by her estranged husband, Paul Snider. The cover, widely seen when first published, was seen even more widely when Stratten was killed, then more widely still when Stratten's story was turned into the movie *Star 80*, with Mariel Hemingway playing Dorothy Stratten, Eric Roberts playing Paul Snider, and Cliff Robertson playing Hugh Hefner. The cover was remade for the movie, with Stratten replaced by Hemingway, but with Herb Cohen's tagline—"Winning Through Negotiation: How to Get What You Want"—in place.

Herbie speaks of the rule of three. If someone sees your name three times—initial publication, murder, movie—they feel as if you're everywhere, so must be famous, and, if people think you're famous, you're famous. He says he finally decided to write a book in 1980 because he wanted to retire some of his older bits and hoped to preserve them when they were still fresh in his mind, and while that's probably true, he must have also felt the wind at his back.

He's big on lecturing his kids and grandkids about study habits, perseverance, and establishing a routine. He told us to go about our work in a methodical and even boring way, to conduct ourselves in the practice exam or scrimmage as if it were the real test or game; that way, when we got there, we'd feel as if we'd already been there a dozen times before. "Don't do anything differently," he'd say. "Make the extraordinary ordinary. That's the key."

But that is not at all how he behaved when he wrote his book. He did not go about it as he'd gone about his earlier work on seminars and speeches—casually, at the kitchen table, a few hours at a time. He did not make the extraordinary ordinary. He made the extraordinary super-extraordinary. He set up a cramped office in the basement, said goodbye one morning, went down there, and stayed down there until he'd finished. Eight months in that hole, forty pots of coffee a day, nothing to eat but lettuce and bread, filling dozens of yellow legal pads with neat cursive in calligraphy pen, composing the book just as it was meant to be read, from open to close, starting with the first sentence: "Your real world is a giant negotiating table, and like it or not, you're a participant."

Then:

> *You, as an individual, come into conflict with others: family members, sales clerks, competitors, or entities with impressive names like "the Establishment" or "the power structure." How you handle these encounters can determine not only whether you prosper, but whether you can enjoy a full, pleasurable, satisfying life.*

Summer came and went. Then Labor Day. The first week of school. The autumn leaves. Halloween and Thanksgiving. *Peanuts* on TV. The first frost. Christmas. Winter storms. Now and then, a cry from the depths: "Ellen! Ellen!" A few air bubbles breaking the surface. Otherwise, nothing. There were days, even weeks, when we almost forgot he was down there.

He was gaunt as a prisoner when he finally emerged. Spring had come. Buds were on the cherry trees—cracking ice, the sound of water. He was dirty and bearded but looked righteous. When he rejoined us, it was in the way of Moses returning with the tablets.

Behold!

Can you imagine a more painful way to write a book? In a single marathon session in a water-damaged suburban basement? Kerouac used Benzedrine. Hemingway drank anisette. De Quincey smoked opium. Hunter S. Thompson dropped LSD. For Herb Cohen, there was nothing but lettuce, bread, and black coffee.

No. 30

NEEDING TO MARK THE OCCASION, HERBIE TOLD ELLEN TO pull the children out of school. He was taking us on a drive. He spread a map on the kitchen table and marked the route. He wanted the trip to mimic the trip he'd just taken in his head. We'd go south to Missouri, then head west for the mountains.

The manuscript—a stack of coffee-stained pages—sat beside him in the car. He planned to read the entire book out loud in the course of the drive. That was the trip's real purpose. He wanted his first audience close and captive so he could gauge each reaction, tell which bits fizzled and which bits landed.

My parents owned a Chrysler Town & Country, a green station wagon with imitation-wood paneling. We folded down the backseats and made a nest of blankets and pillows. We had snacks, video games, Yes & Know invisible-ink books, comics. We left in the dark, Herbie behind the wheel. He took Sheridan Road to Lake Shore Drive, then continued to Interstate 55. The city was on our right, a huge forest of glass and steel. The sun appeared across the lake and lit the towers. The shadows of the tallest buildings—the Hancock and Sears—stretched all the way to Iowa. We descended into a great Gehenna of iron mills and blast furnaces and refineries, the fires burning day and night, the blue flames of chemical smoke, the awesome stacks.

Herbie rolled up his window, put on Sinatra, grinned. Ellen was smiling, too. We followed the interstate through Joliet, famous for its ribs and prison, then continued down the spine of Illinois, factories giving way to towns—Lexington, Bloomington, Lincoln—towns giving way to cornfields that rolled unbroken to the sky.

We got onto I-70 West in Edwardsville, Illinois.

I asked where we were going.

Herbie said, "To the highest peak we can find."

I asked what we'd do when we got there.

He said, "Turn around and come back."

"Why?"

"Because that's life," he said. "You go, you turn around, you come back."

This trip confused me at the time, but now, being older than he was then, I think I know what he was doing. He'd written a book, and in the process the book had changed. What he'd envisioned as a business guide had become his own story. He'd put everything he'd done and learned in that book. And it diminished him. You lose whatever you put on paper. He needed to acknowledge this loss with a dramatic gesture. He needed to put an exclamation point at the end of this chapter of his life.

We crossed the Mississippi River in St. Louis, then continued through Missouri. We were in Kansas City by sundown, rolling through a parking lot, looking for a space so we could go inside and eat barbecue. Ellen drove after dinner so Herbie could read us his book. Maybe that sounds boring, but hearing him read those pages out loud—I hung over the front seat, following along with his loopy handwriting—was exciting. It was hard to believe I knew someone who'd actually written a book.

There was a story about me in the first chapter. It did not matter that it made me out to be a nightmare child. I was in a book! I would live forever! "My wife and I have three children," Herbie read. "At nine, our youngest son weighed fifty pounds, remarkably light for a child his age. Actually, he was an embarrassment to our entire family. I say that because my wife and I like to eat, and our two oldest children have voracious appetites. Then there was this third kid. People would ask us, 'Where did he come from?' or 'Whose kid is that?'"

The story was meant to illustrate how even a person as seemingly powerless as a scrawny fourth grader can get what he wants. Taken against my strenuous objections to a fancy restaurant for dinner, I'd made a public spectacle, crawling under the table, then, when admonished, standing on a chair and shouting, "This is a crummy restaurant!"

"Startled though I was, I had enough presence of mind to grab him by the neck, shove him back under the table, and ask for the check," Herbie continued. "On the way home, my wife said to me, 'Herb, I think we learned something tonight. Let's not ever take the little monster to a restaurant again.'

"What our nine-year-old did on that embarrassing occasion was use information and power to affect our behavior. Like so many of today's youngsters, he's a negotiator—at least with his parents."

Herbie read a hundred pages as we crossed Kansas. I absorbed every word. I'd always loved the way he talked about biblical figures, as if they were modern humans: "Jesus Christ and Socrates . . . were negotiators. They were Win-Win ethical negotiators, and they were power people." I loved the way he revealed small acts of control that go unnoticed, like price tags in department stores: "It's no ordinary sign scrawled with Magic Marker. It's symmetrical and professionally done: block printed on expensive chipboard. And it appears to have been placed there by the Big Printer in the Sky." I loved the way he reversed the negative so you could see an old picture in a new way: "Don't regard yourself as someone who wants to buy a refrigerator. Regard yourself as someone who wants to sell money. Money is the product that's up for sale. The more people there are who want your money, the more your money will buy. How do you get people to bid for that money? You generate competition."

I loved the way he returned to a few cardinal rules, the sort that apply not just to business but to life, because, as he'd say, "it's never about business; it's always about life."

"Who's the worst person to negotiate for?

"Yourself.

"You do a much better job negotiating for someone else.

"Why?

"Because you take yourself too seriously in any interaction that concerns *you*. You care too much about yourself. That puts you under pressure and stress. When you negotiate for someone else, you're more relaxed. You're more objective. You don't care as much, because you regard the situation as fun or a game—*which it is*."

He wrote just the way he talked, with wisecracks and asides. You could hear the accents and shtick. There was something funny and smart on just about every page. He began each chapter with a quotation: "Some people feel the rain; others just get wet" (Roger Miller); "If you think you can or can't, you're right" (Henry Ford I); "As long as you get there before it's over you're never late" (James J. Walker).

I loved his chapter titles, too. "Weakness as a Strength." "We Don't Understand." "The Power of Risk Taking." And the way he ended each section with a message or a big idea. "Never see anyone as an isolated unit. See those whom you wish to persuade in context, as a central core around which others move. Get the support of those others and you will influence the position and movement of the core." Or: "Keep saying to yourself over and over, 'It's a game. It's the world of illusion. A tactic perceived is no tactic. I care, but not that much.'" Or: "The good life is not a passive existence where you live and let live. It's one of involvement where you live and help live."

We spent the night at a motel in Goodland, Kansas, had breakfast at Bob's Big Boy in the morning, then continued, my mother still driving. When people think of Colorado, they think of mountains, but the eastern part of the state is as flat as a griddle, which meant long views from the back of the station wagon: wheat fields and grain elevators, fat cows and billowy clouds, and a real-life cowboy on a speckled horse.

We opened the windows. The air was cool and dry. The Rockies appeared as a jagged line against the sky. We drove south along the eastern front of the mountains, then took the plunge. We were headed for Pikes Peak. We could see the summit from miles away, white and dazzling. Herbie told us about the mountain as Ellen drove: fourteen thousand feet above sea level, holy to the Ute Indians and holy still, the attic of the world.

A two-lane road went up, each switchback opening on an abyss that made your stomach drop. The temperature fell as we climbed; the wind picked up. The car was soon being slammed by the wind. There were dark clouds in the west, far away but moving fast.

Herbie turned on the heat and smiled at Ellen, who was not smiling. She gripped the steering wheel, white knuckling it. Herbie had finished reading his book, and that's what he was thinking about—not the mountain, or the abyss, or the possibility of a fiery crash, but his work. He believed it was good, possibly very good, and it was this belief, which never wavered, that would give him the confidence to persist despite

the rejections that were coming. Quoting Harry Truman, he'd
say, "I make a decision once." And he'd made his decision
about the book. In case of rejection, the only thing that would
change was his opinion of the publishing house.

There was a cafeteria and a gift shop on top of the mountain; there's often a gift shop on top of the mountain. We ate
at the buffet, bought postcards in the store, then got back in
the car. From here on, Herbie did the driving. The storm had
arrived while we were eating. Snow roared from the west, the
road slick and black, the weather worsening by the minute.
We could see flashes of lightning in the clouds. Herbie slowed
first to fifteen, then to five, then to two miles an hour. Ice
covered the windshield. He leaned out and cleared an opening. He was like a submarine captain, steering by periscope.
There were cars on the side of the road. Some drivers had
skidded off the pavement. Some had pulled over to wait out
the storm. Some were fitting their tires with chains. Herbie
continued, chainless and arrogant, confident he could get us
down. We could not see beyond the shoulder, but knew the
cliffs were there.

Ellen suddenly screamed, "I don't care what happens to
me! I just don't want the children to die!"

Herbie looked at her, then laughed.

"Bullshit," he said. "It's you. You don't want to die."

The sky was clear when we got back to the highway. There
was a beautiful sunset. It was as if the storm never happened.
The rest of the drive was like the victorious drumroll at the
end of an Aaron Copland symphony. It was winter, then
spring, the countryside blooming as we passed through it, as
if our passage were what made it bloom.

No. 31

ELLEN TYPED HERBIE'S HANDWRITTEN MANUSCRIPT, MADE copies, then helped Herbie assemble a list of publishers, ordered by perceived prestige, first to last. He started with Simon & Schuster, then, when rejected, made his way through the list. As another writer once said of his early submissions, "They came back faster than Ping-Pong balls." Some with a handwritten note—"Thank you, not for us"; "Interesting in places but too special"—most with a form letter. If the stress of the experience—send, wait, wait, wait, rejected—weighed on Herbie, and it must have, he didn't show it. The man has a genius for sheltering his family and himself from every kind of bad weather—inner and outer. When Ellen asked how he could sleep so soundly in the midst of bad times, he said, "I put each one of my troubles in a cubbyhole; then, when I'm done for the day, I close the door to each of those cubbyholes."

He never stopped believing he would find a publisher. "It only takes one," he'd say. "Then, when the book hits, all those rejections will just make for a better story."

It took eighteen noes to get to yes, which came from a strange one-of-a-kinder named Lyle Stuart, a burly, bearded independent with an office in Secaucus, New Jersey. Stuart had edited and published every kind of author and every kind of book, had gone, as Sinatra sang, "from neighborhood saloons to Carnegie Hall." He was a controversial figure, a muscle car running on fumes, by the time Herbie found him. He had both a taste for gossip and an instinct for the mainstream. He knew what people actually wanted as opposed to what they said or thought they wanted. He'd started in newspaper tabloids, first as a reporter, then as a publisher. He was a founder of the showbiz rag *Private Eye*. After winning eight thousand dollars in a libel suit against the columnist Walter Winchell, he used the money to open a publishing company, where he promised to take on whatever interested him without fear. He described himself as the "last publisher in America with any guts" and scored hits with titles other companies would never touch: *The Sensuous Woman, Inside the F.B.I., The Anarchist Cookbook*, which included directions (recipes) for how to make guns and bombs.

While most publishers operated within a closed professional circle, Lyle Stuart kept his eye on the mail. He was interested in what came in from the outside, the vast accumulation of unsolicited manuscripts known in the industry as the slush pile. You never know what the postman might bring. Stuart recognized a kindred spirit first in Herbie's book, then in Herbie himself. Here was another New York kid raised far from the establishment, another intruder, another immigrant's son at once inside and outside, with the distance to diagnose the ills and meet the needs of a greater public.

Lyle Stuart read the book, then talked to Herbie on the phone, then flew to Chicago with a contract. He sat at our kitchen table watching my father sign. In his excitement and relief, Herbie violated one of his own rules: "Never negotiate for yourself." It's ironic that in agreeing to terms for the publication of *You Can Negotiate Anything*, Herb Cohen, whom *Playboy* had dubbed "the world's best negotiator," sort of got taken. There was a small advance and a less than generous royalty split. But at that moment, Herbie would have done almost anything to see his book in print.

Why?

Because he cared too much!

The book did not have a name. I remember Herbie experimenting with various titles—*Win-Win*; *Power Negotiation*; *If You Don't Know Where You're Going, Any Road Will Get You There*—before coming up with one he really liked. It's said that a good book title should make a promise. Well, if that's true, I'd argue that Herbie had concocted the greatest book title of all time. Including subtitle, it makes not one but *two* hugely outlandish promises: *You Can Negotiate Anything: How to Get What You Want*.

Lyle Stuart hired a photographer to take Herbie's picture for the back cover. The familiarity of this picture, the fact that I know it the way I know the Nike swoop, obscures just how in-your-face it is. Herb Cohen, slim and handsome at forty-seven, Seiko watch and three-piece suit, fists on hips, a personification of power not because he is big and strong, nor because he knows more than you do, but because "power is based on perception." Here is a salesman, not of cars, houses, or life insurance, but of the secret to mastering your fate.

The front cover was so simple—red and orange letters on a white background—it seemed either half-baked or brilliant. We received our first copy a few weeks before publication. It came like a baby to parents who've been told they cannot conceive—that kind of miracle, that kind of joy. We held it up to the light, smelled the binding, flipped through the pages, looked for our names, read them out loud, looked at the author photo, then placed it on a shelf between the Bible and *The Big Book of Jewish Humor*.

The acknowledgments stirred up trouble in the extended family. It wasn't that Herbie thanked neither my sister, my brother, nor myself, though he'd made liberal use of our lives, that rankled, but the fact that he didn't mention the Eisenstadts. This small thing came up again and again over the years. For Gladys and Betty, it was like a bone in the throat. (I never knew what Ben really thought about anything.) Especially galling to Betty was the fact that in addition to Saul Alinsky, Viktor Frankl, and George F. Kennan, Herbie thanked Francis Albert Sinatra. I could hear it from across the room as she scolded my mother on the phone, saying, "We've done more for your husband than Frank Sinatra."

Presented with this *j'accuse*, Herbie thought a moment, then asked, "But have they?"

You Can Negotiate Anything was published in early September. Lyle Stuart manufactured and distributed the books, but sales and marketing were left largely to Herbie, who considered himself a master at moving product. "Life is ninety-seven percent marketing," he'd say. "You're better off with a mediocre product and a great salesman than with a masterpiece and an idiot to sell it."

Herbie broke the book the way Sammy the Bull broke arms—by hand. "Send two hundred and fifty copies," he told Lyle Stuart, "and leave the rest to me." He loaded the boxes into the station wagon on a Sunday night and set off by himself at dawn. Every American city had its own media in the 1980s, its own television morning shows, its own evening news, its own newspapers and magazines. Herbie set up at a hotel in each new city—Cincinnati, Omaha, Des Moines, Buffalo—got on the phone, and started making calls to producers, editors, writers. In this way, he got himself interviewed on radio and TV, written up in newspapers, featured in magazines. His aphorisms had been polished to a high shine. "A man with a big canoe has big problems, a man with a small canoe has small problems." "To get to the promised land, you have to negotiate your way through the wilderness."

He had become a Jewish Buddha, preaching detachment.

He went into every bookstore he could find, moved his book to the front, the top of the display, then signed every copy—he did this without being asked—beginning each inscription, "Congratulations. Merely by picking up this book, you have demonstrated your intelligence."

The book was selling long before he realized it, driven by word of mouth, dog-eared and marked up, borrowed, left on a train, purchased again. First mention of sales came in articles in local papers, often accompanied by a photo of Herbie. Thousands of copies had sold, then tens of thousands, then tens of tens of thousands. It went into a second, third, fourth, fifth, sixth . . . nineteenth printing. In a movie, you'd see copies pouring off factory belts. It was a local bestseller, then a regional bestseller, then a national bestseller.

Herbie, keen on intelligence collection (he advises anyone desiring success to seek time, information, and power, or TIP) sent me into dozens of Chicago-area stores to ask about *You Can Negotiate Anything—Where is it in the store? How many copies do you have in stock? How is it selling? Do you have more on order?*—without revealing my connection to the author.

"What if they ask why I want it?" (I was in eighth grade.)
"Tell them it's a gift, or that you're interested in negotiation."

I felt a rush of pride at our local mall, Northbrook Court, when the woman at the counter smiled and said, "It was written by Glencoe's *own* Herb Cohen."

It was number two on the *Chicago Sun-Times* bestseller list. It was number one in the *Tribune*. It was at the top of every list in the country with the maddening exception of *The New York Times*, a fact that nearly eclipsed all the success in Herbie's mind. He's a New Yorker, and to him nothing's been achieved until it's been achieved in New York.

He pestered Lyle Stuart. How can a book be on every other bestseller list in the country and not be in the *Times*? It makes no sense! As it happened, the *Times Book Review* editors, not expecting anything from Lyle Stuart or Herb Cohen, had not been tracking *You Can Negotiate Anything*. To them, it was as if it did not exist. And what doesn't exist can't be counted. As soon as they did begin to track it—Stuart raised a stink—it appeared near the top, then began climbing. Number six. Number four. Number three. Like every writer in America, Herbie dreamed of being number one in the *Times*. He reached number two, then stayed there for weeks, stalled an inch from the finish line. As Herbie says, you might be the jack of hearts, but the ace of spades is somewhere in the deck, which, in this case, was *Cosmos* by Carl Sagan, which spent more than a year at the top, blocking all access to number one.

The success of the book affected my life in many ways. Now, whenever I disagreed with a teacher at school, she'd cut me off, saying, "You can't negotiate everything in this class,

Mr. Cohen." When I picked up Becky Goodman on my bike for an eighth-grade dance, her father sat me down, asked what I planned to do with my life, then made a big joke about how he hoped I wasn't planning to use any of my father's "slick techniques" on his daughter that night. He reprised this joke years later at Becky's wedding, where, in the big toast, he said, "She once dated the kid of that guy who wrote *You Can Negotiate Anything* . . ."

How else did the book affect me?

When I was in eighth grade, a lump appeared just below my stomach, near my waistband. It didn't hurt, but seemed ominous. When I showed it to my mother, she dismissed it as psychosomatic.

"In other words," I said, "you believe I have created this lump with my mind."

"Yes."

Herbie called this diagnosis nuts, then got out a big old medical encyclopedia. He checked the index for my symptoms, flipped through the pages, read a passage, then, putting the book back, said, "You have a hernia." When I went to the doctor, he noticed an infected wound on my leg, which I'd burned while riding on the back of a motorcycle. He said the infection had caused an inflammation in a gland, and that was the lump. He prescribed antibiotics. Once the infection clears, he said, the lump will go away. The doctor laughed when I told him my father thought I had a hernia, then said, "Why don't we leave the negotiating to the negotiators and the doctoring to the doctors." The antibiotics cleared up the infection, but the lump remained. When I went back to Dr. Lippman, he examined me a second time, then said,

"Well, I'll be damned. The negotiator was right. You do have a hernia."

No. 32

HERBIE LOST TOUCH WITH MOST OF THE WARRIORS OVER the years. We knew their names from the stories—Bucko, Who Ha, Inky—but they were no more than legends, punch lines, characters in a book. He followed Larry's career in the press, though, because Larry became famous almost as soon as he left Bensonhurst.

He'd taken a train to Miami Beach one afternoon at the end of the 1950s. He'd dreamed of working in radio and heard the industry was wide open in Florida. He got a job at a midsize station that catered to a young audience. Talk shows in the morning, music at night. He handed out newspapers, went for coffee, cleaned up the studio. He stood on a balcony between errands, smoking a cigarette as he looked down at the palm trees and motels, neon light in the morning, Cadillacs on Ocean Drive. Miami Beach was the winter capital of New York café society in the 1960s. The *schvitzes* were filled with grandparents; the nightclubs were filled with pop idols, Frank Sinatra and Buddy Hackett, Johnny Stompanato with Lana Turner on his arm, Jerry and Dino bickering at the back bar.

Larry made a study of the talent at the station, the talk show hosts and record spinners. Everyone knew he wanted to be on air. It's all he talked about. He worked on his delivery as he wandered the office, calming himself with the mantra

"And here we go, folks, from the top of the charts!" He was bucktoothed at twenty-five, eyes shrunken to pinpricks behind the thick lenses of his horn-rimmed frames. Sometimes a cliché can be useful: Larry did indeed have a perfect face for radio. But his voice was top-notch, an authoritative baritone that put listeners into a trance. A voice like that is akin to a hundred-mile-an-hour fastball. You can show a kid how to throw a curve, but you can't teach speed.

The program director called Larry into his office one afternoon.

"The night guy took a powder," he said. "You're going on. What's your name?"

"Larry."

"Your full name."

"Larry Zeiger."

"Nah. Too Brooklyn. Too Jewish."

He looked at his desk, where a copy of the *Racing Form* was open to the winners at the local track. Tapping an ad at the bottom of the page—a surfer with a cigarette over the words "Tastes Great, Smokes Mild—Chesterfield KING!"—he said, "From now on you're Larry King."

Larry's debut was rocky in the classic way; that's how myths begin, David fumbling with the pebble, Lou Gehrig tripping over the bats. A record was playing when Larry took over in the studio, where it was dim and cool, always night. He lifted the needle on Dean Martin's "That's Amore" and turned to the microphone to introduce Jo Stafford's "You Belong to Me," but nothing came out. He was dumbstruck, frozen. He dropped the needle back on Dino, let the song play for a few seconds, then tried again, failed, then tried again. It took five attempts to find his voice, by which time the program director was glaring in the doorway.

Larry Zeiger was a clod, but Larry King was a natural. Despite the rough start, he was good early and got better fast. He'd soon replaced the all-night deejay, then moved to mornings, then landed his own talk show, where his arcane knowledge and gift for street corner gab made him a Miami Beach star. He moved his show to Pumpernik's delicatessen on Collins Avenue, where, five days a week, he interviewed whatever performer or celebrity happened to be in town. If he did not have a guest, he'd talk to people hanging around in the deli, or he'd just talk. Unlike other interviewers, he did not care how he came across. He was willing to look silly, even ridiculous, in an attempt to get answers to the sorts of questions a regular person would ask. *Were you scared? What's she like in the sack? How much money do you make for a thing like that?* He was shameless but without guile. Honest. He really did want to know what it was like to sleep with Elizabeth Taylor. He really did believe Frank Sinatra could tell him who'd killed John Kennedy. Jackie Gleason appeared on his show, as did Judy Garland, Danny Kaye, Danny Thomas, Lucille Ball, Robert Mitchum, J. Edgar Hoover, Richard Nixon, and Bebe Rebozo. Lenny Bruce walked by the front window of Pumpernik's in a striped prison outfit, as if he'd just busted out of the joint. Larry broadcast the scene as Bruce stopped a cop and asked for "the quickest way out of town."

Larry lived on a houseboat in the Intracoastal Waterway, dated bunnies from the Playboy Club, and bet horses. He'd always had a gambling problem but hadn't had the money to get into real trouble. Now that he did, he spent most of his free time at Hialeah, the big track in Miami-Dade County. The names of the horses, the odds, the action around the pari-mutuel window, the low-level mobsters and the wads they carried, the way they talked—he couldn't get enough of it. He sat with the big shots and the touts in the grandstand, forever in search of tips, the inside skinny on the next race.

One Friday afternoon, the owner of the radio station asked Larry to drop off that week's revenue at the bank. Larry looked in the envelope when he was alone; there was a stack of hundred-dollar bills in there, maybe fifty grand in C-notes. Larry sat in his car for twenty minutes, looking at the money, thinking. Then he drove to the track. He'd gotten a tip on a horse, a sure thing. And he bet it all. He would've pocketed close to a million dollars if he'd won, but he didn't win. The horse stumbled coming out of the third turn—there was mud in the air, its eyes were wild. The way he felt when he lost that money was the worst and also the best part of gambling for Larry, the terror, the adrenaline. You never feel more alive than when you are truly screwed. Larry was left a single option—run like hell! He stopped by his houseboat, packed a bag, got in his car, and went north. Miami Beach was soon behind him, Jews and bookies and a perfectly good career fading in the rearview mirror.

The bank manager called the station owner—*we're still waiting for the deposit.* The station owner tried to find Larry, then called the Miami Beach police, who called the state police, who put out an arrest warrant. Larry was pulled over on Highway 1, ninety-five miles north of Miami. He'd been heading for Brooklyn, returning, in the way of an exotic animal, to his nesting ground to hide. His mug shot is an artifact of twentieth-century showbiz lore. You see desperation in those black eyes. His pockets are empty, and his thoughts have been pared to just one: *survive.* The sound in his head was the roar of the sea. You can learn more from a mug shot than from a hundred photos taken on the red-carpet. Frank Sinatra looks young in his mug shot, floppy-haired, defiant. Though jonesing for amphetamines, Johnny Cash still looks

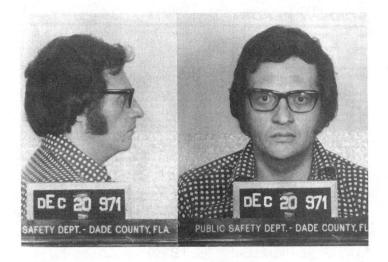

tough in his. John Belushi is doing that eyebrow thing. Elvis Presley might have been snared, but he's still the King. Kurt Cobain looks like the kid caught pulling a high school fire alarm. Larry looks empty. You see it and think, "Oh, so that's what they mean by rock bottom."

The station owner, understanding that Larry was a weak, temptation-driven character—not a criminal, just a schmuck—

dropped the charges. Larry, who agreed to return the money as soon as he had it, was free, but free to do what? He was out of a houseboat, out of a career. He did not visit Miami Beach again for years. Nor did he go to Brooklyn. The story of his arrest had made national news, and he was too ashamed to show his face.

If Herbie had been in Larry's life, it never would've happened; he would've gotten Larry out of it just as he'd gotten him out of the Moppo thing, just as he'd gotten Tommy DeLuca out of the trouble with army intelligence. He tried, calling every person and number he could think of in an effort to contact Larry, but Larry did not want to be contacted. He'd made himself vanish. He was like a jumbo jet that one minute is blazing across a clear sky and is gone the next. As if he'd never existed. As if he'd never been born. As if he'd been sent to purgatory, where he'd pay for his sins with a fate he feared more than death—obscurity.

And so I sing the song of Zeke the Creek's Missing Years.

He retrieved his car and headed west. He slept in motor courts and ate in diners, swam in hotel pools surrounded by chain-link fence, lingered in faded beach towns with arcades. Pensacola. Destin. Fort Walton. The Florida Panhandle is like the bottom of the sea. When he looked back at Miami, he saw an angel with a flaming sword barring his return. He spent his last dollar on a pack of cigarettes in Biloxi, Mississippi, then noticed a 50-watt radio station that broadcast local news and high school sports. He went inside and got a job.

Because he was so good on the air, he was noticed and promoted. He moved to a bigger station in Mobile, Alabama. He also worked at trade shows, called college baseball games, and hung out in local nightspots. He continued on to Louisiana, first Shreveport, then Lafayette, then Alexandria, a small city in the middle of the state. He worked on a station in the afternoon and called the greyhound races at the dog track at night. He met a woman. They lived together in a ranch house on the nicest street in town. He could smell magnolia flowers as he stood over the Weber grill. He'd formed new habits, wore strange clothes, made new friends. He joined a country club and became a college football aficionado. It was almost like amnesia, the emptiness that allowed him to operate without thought of the past.

He was approached at the dog track by a station manager from New Orleans who'd heard Larry while sitting in the grandstand. He still had that voice. To find him announcing greyhound races in Alexandria was like finding Nolan Ryan pitching on a sandlot. He offered Larry a job. A month later, Larry was once again working at a major station. Once again, he was given a talk show. Once again, celebrities and writers and politicians found their way to him. Once again, he was famous.

In 1977, he signed a deal with Mutual Broadcasting, a radio network carried by over five hundred affiliates. He moved to suburban D.C., leaving everything behind, even the woman in his life. (He'd be married nine times before it was all over, a fact that embarrassed Larry but that Herbie explained by saying, "Larry doesn't believe in premarital sex.") The road Larry had followed from the time he'd made bail in Florida led back to his original road, making the years between seem like nothing more than an unreal detour, a fantastic dream. Sometimes, when he tried to think back on his life in Louisiana—the woman, the friends, the Weber grill—he could hardly believe it had happened.

The Larry King Show on Mutual Broadcasting became a cult sensation. Millions tuned in each night from 11:05 p.m. to 4:00 a.m. For the nocturnal, the law students and truckers, the gas station attendants and short-order cooks, the firemen and cops who inhabited the nighttime world, Larry was a godsend, a voice to talk you through the wee hours. His show was a solace to insomniacs. Just knowing you were not alone, that Larry was also awake, made it easier.

There was a guest for the first few hours of the show, then Larry told stories or took calls, a segment known as "Open Phone America." He interviewed every sort of expert and celebrity on his show, politicians and athletes, mentalists and UFO abductees. Comedians would call in at two or three in the morning to try new material. And Larry told stories . . . about the Warriors, about Moppo, about Carvel and three scoops for fifteen cents. Most of these stories featured Herbie. He talked about the time Herbie confessed to a crime he did not commit—"because if you ask me a question, I tell you the truth twice, but if you don't believe me and ask a third time, I tell you whatever you want to hear"—and about the time Herbie, on the mound before a game at Yankee Stadium with Larry and other kids from the Police Athletic League, told the great pitcher Billy Pierce that he was using the wrong grip on his curveball. "Actually, the kid is right," said Pierce.

When Herbie and Larry reconnected, it was as if no time had passed. Larry was living in Alexandria, Virginia, with his new wife, number three. Herbie was restless. Having finished his book, he was eagerly awaiting publication. Larry's stories had already made Herbie famous to a population of late-night radio fanatics. Larry called and asked Herbie to come on the air and tell those stories from his point of view. Herbie and Larry had so much fun on the show, and it was such a hit with listeners, they decided to do it again a few weeks later. Then did it again. Herbie made more appearances when his book was published. Having told all the old stories, Herbie and Larry began inventing characters, routines—street corner shtick. One night, after talking for a few hours about negotiation, Herbie said goodnight, then returned as an extraterrestrial named Gork from the planet Fringus, his voice scrambled by a synthesizer. The ET had a thick Brooklyn accent.

Fringus was located in a galactic system ninety days ahead of earth, meaning that Gork, with his magnificent eyesight, could look across the void and see what was happening on our planet three months hence. These were not predictions; they were facts. Callers asked about the future, and Gork told them. Herbie and Larry gave up the routine when they realized people were actually making life and death decisions—cancer surgery, yes or no?—based on Gork. One night, hours after I was supposed to be asleep, I called the show and asked Gork where I'd be in three months. "I see you in a dark place," said Gork. "Very dark. It's a box. You're in a box being sent to Lima, Peru."

No. 33

LARRY BECAME A REGULAR PRESENCE IN OUR LIVES. WE were sent to his house on school vacations. He visited Glencoe, making camp in the back bedroom, staying weeks at a

time. I could hear him laughing in the kitchen as I fell asleep and talking in the kitchen when I opened my eyes in the morning.

Ellen had not liked Larry Zeiger and did not like Larry King. As far as she was concerned, a schmuck by any other name is still a schmuck.

Herbie used to say this thing when he didn't like one of my friends: "You sustain a loss of brain tissue just by being around that person." That's how Ellen felt about Larry. She felt shunted aside when he was around, like a third wheel, on the outside looking in and not liking what she saw. To her Larry was a cad who did not regard women as full members of the human race.

There were times she worried that she was losing my father. Not just to Larry, but to success, fame, opportunity, a wider world. She had my sister to confide in; then my sister left for college. She had my brother; then he went to NYU. After that, with Herbie on the road most of the time, it was just me and my mom at 1062 Bluff Road. We watched a lot of old movies together. I drank Coke. She took Valium. Only later did I realize that she was not always happy. A New Yorker to the core, she did not like Chicago, and liked its suburbs even less. She was scared to drive in the snow, which kept her inside from November until April. She hated to drive in the dark in any season, claiming she suffered from a condition called night blindness. Unsettled by non-domesticated wildlife, she was home alone when a raccoon gave birth in the attic, when a crow dropped through the chimney into the living room, when a squirrel hopped past her and into the house while she was signing for a package.

She spent years in analysis trying to determine the source of her unease, though I could have explained it in a minute. It was her parents, who, in attempting to appease mad Gladys, had neglected their younger daughter.

By the time I was in high school, Gladys was less person than caricature, a stand-in for the general nastiness of the world. She'd taken to her bed before I started grade school, and it was in that bed that she fell apart, that her hands knotted, her face puckered, her joints failed. She was like Rapunzel if Rapunzel never escaped the tower. She had turned herself into a cripple by force of will, forfeited her life, then blamed it on Ellen. She convinced herself that Ellen had taken her place, that it was not the Fall of man but the birth of Ellen that brought misery into the world. Whatever had gone right for Ellen had been taken from Gladys, and whatever had gone wrong for Gladys properly belonged to Ellen. She tormented her parents with this delusion. She wanted to turn them against Ellen the way a prosecutor flips a witness, which she was able to do because, while Ellen was far away, Gladys was always close and never stropped bitching.

Ellen was constantly worried about being denounced by Gladys and betrayed by Betty and Ben. Herbie reassured her every time she got off the phone with her parents, which of course caused Herbie to resent his in-laws, which is probably what Gladys wanted. She created a crack, then hammered at it. She told Ellen to stop calling because Betty did not want to hear from her, then told Betty that Ellen didn't call because Ellen didn't love her. "She quit you, Ma. And you should quit her, too."

Though confined to bed, Gladys could be dangerous. She had a violent temper. She threw dishes, punched walls, smashed remote controls. She'd hit her grandmother when she was young and hit Betty when she was old. If contradicted, she'd scream, "You should rot in hell for what you said to me!"

For years, I thought my mother had been exaggerating. I did not blame her. She'd been hurt, treated unfairly, and, in her anger, had lost perspective. Nobody has the critical distance to judge their own family; that truth is the bedrock beneath Herbie's rule against negotiating for yourself. When it came to Gladys, Ellen cared too much to be objective. I mean, come on, how could anyone be that bad?

One example: My mother told me that, though she'd tried to repair her relationship with Gladys, "having our telephone bugged was the last straw."

Me: "Wait. Stop. What do you mean, 'having our telephone bugged'?"

Ellen: "Your aunt Gladys had a bug put on our phone. I kept hearing clicking on the line, static or interference. The calls sounded funny. Your father said I was crazy. Then he heard it, too. He asked an FBI friend to look into it. He told us we had a bug, that it had been put there by a private security company and paid for by Cumberland"—the Eisenstadt family business.

Though I nodded as my mother told this story, I figured she'd either misunderstood or conflated two people—Nixon and Gladys—and was in possession of what psychiatrists call a false memory. Then, in 2006, while working on my book *Sweet and Low*, I interviewed Gladys in her room in Midwood. When trying to explain the family rift as it appeared from Glencoe, I said, "Distance can create misunderstanding, and my mom could be a little paranoid. For example, she actually believed you had our telephone tapped."

"Well, I had to!" Gladys shot back. "I knew Ellen was talking about me, and I had to hear what she was saying. Pop said she'd never find out, but of course she did, and she'd never let it go."

Hence the paranoia that occasionally overwhelmed my mother. To quote Henry Kissinger, "Even paranoiacs have real enemies." When it came on, it came on like a flu, this fever, this dread sense that someone was out to get her. She treated these episodes with various tonics over the years, with each treatment defining a period of my adolescence: the yellow period (Valium), the clear period (vodka), the loquacious period (psychotherapy).

Psychotherapy gave her a new language, fresh words to describe her predicament. It gave her a story to tell about herself, a story that let her view her life from a distance, as if it were that of a stranger, which was a relief. She called these sessions, which took place in an office downtown, "the work." "'The work' is exhilarating," she'd say, "but exhausting." When "the work" had gone well, she'd come home with tears in her eyes, smile, and say, "It's not my fault. It was never my fault." There were bad days, too, when she returned to the house as limp as a rag. "Just when you think you've reached the end of 'the work,'" she'd say, taking the Stoli out of the freezer, "it starts again."

Ellen wore oversize prescription sunglasses throughout the 1970s and 1980s. These gave her the appearance of a comely cartoon bug. She wore pantsuits and frilly blouses. She'd been coloring her hair—it had turned gray in college— since she'd been in her twenties. It was styled twice a month by a beautician named Dennis, who liked to experiment, who liked to "play." She usually wore it short and brown with frosted tips, but now and then she'd return from an appointment with Dennis as a redhead or blonde, and when this happened, I experienced a kind of vertigo. Not recognizing her at first, I'd ask myself, "Who am I? Where is this?"

She tended to experience "breakthroughs" in the first few months with a new therapist; she'd tell us what she'd learned in excited tones. The pace of the revelations would slow, then stop. If she changed hair color, it meant she'd hit a therapeutic wall. She wanted to be understood and loved, and tended to co-opt her therapists in this effort, turn them from doctors into friends. I can date weddings by the presence of a particular analyst in the photo album. If Dr. Marks is in the conga line, it's Sharon's wedding. If Dr. Solomon is by the cake, it's Steven's.

She quit psychiatry in favor of self-treatment via the bookstore self-help section. That's what the Reagan years, a boom time for recovered memories, life-changing diets, and energy-infusing aerobic regimens, were all about: bootstrapping body and soul into a better you. The covers of these books linger in the mind like the faces of old friends who did not keep their promises: *The Power of Now*; *The Road Less Traveled*; *What Color Is Your Parachute?*; *If You Meet the Buddha on the Road, Kill Him*; *I'm OK, You're OK*. Ellen was especially enamored of a book on self-hypnosis. She'd read a paragraph, set down the book, close her eyes, breathe deep—in through the nose, out through the mouth—then start to count.

During this phase, Herbie and Ellen took a flight from Denver to Sun Valley, Idaho, a short hop over the mountains on the sort of small fixed-wing aircraft in which the passengers can see the pilots at work. The plane—there were no more than a dozen passengers—ran into serious turbulence. Herbie watched the pilot talk to the co-pilot as Ellen read her book on self-hypnosis. The plane began a steep ascent. "It felt like we were going straight up," Herbie said later. "Then, all of a sudden, I started getting really drowsy."

He looked around. Every other passenger on the plane was asleep, including Ellen, the book in her lap. The pilot and co-pilot had put on oxygen masks. Herbie tried to stay awake, but couldn't. The wheels hitting the runway—BAM!—is what woke him up. His mouth was dry. He had a bad headache. But Ellen was grinning. She said, "This self-hypnosis really works!"

Herbie dealt with Ellen's depression in creative ways, the

most productive being travel. "If you're unhappy here," he'd say, "go somewhere else." He believed two days in a hotel with room service can fix almost anything. Whenever he heard about a high-profile suicide, he'd say, "Why didn't he just get in a car and drive?"

"You might be socked in by fog in Chicago," he'd explain, "but, believe me, the sun is still up there." He told us about a flight he took out of O'Hare during a nasty cold front in February: when the 727 got into the blue sky above the clouds, the passengers cheered.

Whenever Ellen went into a spiral, he'd send us to a friend's house, take his wife to the airport, and buy two tickets to just about anywhere—Santa Fe, New Mexico; Quito, Ecuador—as long as it was different. He took pictures on these trips, then, in the weeks after their return, framed one of these pictures and added it to the gallery he'd assembled on the front table. Most of them showed Ellen in a big hat, a tropical wind blowing, bug-eyed glasses reflecting palm fronds and boulevards. He'd lead her into that hall when she got down, gesture to the menagerie, and say, "How can you be upset? Look at all the amazing places you've been! You're really having a very wonderful life."

There were trips to Israel, where we had relatives. Though

these trips were supposed to be about family and faith, they were really about fights—me against my brother and sister, my sister and me against my brother, my brother and me against my sister, everyone against everyone. It was like a Rubik's Cube with all the possible combinations. Ellen would scream at us to stop. When I decided to punish my parents by keeping my eyes closed in the cable car on the way up Masada, Herbie sat next to me and said, "You know where we're going next year? We're going to pack the bags and go to the basement—you'll see all the same stuff."

Herbie, finally thinking like the author of *You Can Negotiate Anything*, diverted our endless feuding into a more productive channel, setting up a family court that was in session every night after dinner. Herbie was the judge; Ellen was the jury. Witnesses could be questioned under oath, with Herbie reminding each witness of their proximity to the Western Wall. I still have copies of the court dockets, indictments, and subpoenas. In one, "Richard Cohen" charges "Steven Cohen" with "Abuse of a Brother" and "Assault in a Moving Vehicle." In response, "Steven Cohen" charges "Richard Cohen" with "Attempted Murder," then, in his defense, calls a friend from Glencoe, Skip Adamson, to testify, requesting Mr. Adamson be flown to Jerusalem or the charges be dropped.

And of course there were trips to New York to see family and visit the neighborhoods where our parents grew up. These trips were essential for my mother's mental health. At sea in the Midwest, she craved the city as a whaler craves citrus. New York was the only place that seemed entirely real to her. We Cohens of Glencoe lived in a kind of double exile. Like all Jews, we'd been exiled from Jerusalem in the second century. But in 1963, we'd been exiled again, this time from the capital of the diaspora. In Illinois, Herbie and Ellen were like strangers in a strange land, filled with longing. Everything in my childhood was presented as second tier, not quite right. When I ordered a corned beef sandwich at Harrie's Delicatessen in Glencoe, Herbie waited until I'd swallowed a bite, then said, "That sandwich is better in New York." When Tevye came onstage in *Fiddler on the Roof* at the Goodman Theatre in Chicago, he whispered, "This is not the real Tevye. The real Tevye is in New York."

In other words, the New York trips were not vacation but indoctrination. We stayed in a hotel in Manhattan, parents in one room, kids in another—two beds plus a rollaway. We'd walk for hours in the city, which was not the same city I came to know as an adult. It was hotter, more chaotic. There was always a vent blowing in your face. There were always bums on the street. The newsstands were filled with dirty magazines. Times Square was crammed with electronics shops and arcades that went back on forever. Stepping into one of those arcades was like stepping into the wardrobe in the C. S. Lewis book. You never knew where or when you were going to emerge.

Herbie took us to a Chinese restaurant where we were served an exact replica of the meal Nixon and Mao shared during their historic 1972 summit in the Great Hall of the People in Beijing. It consisted of thirty-two distinct courses, including dumplings, Peking duck, fried rice, shark fin soup, and pork garnished with slices of pineapple. Then we went to see *A Chorus Line*. Or *West Side Story*. Or *They're Playing Our Song*. Or *Deathtrap*. We saw several plays during every visit.

Herbie had attended dozens of shows—cheap tickets were part of the GI Bill—in his twenties. He considered the theater a key part of a complete education, a part of life's curriculum in which his children, having been raised in the sticks, were dangerously deficient.

In my first year after college, when I was living on Sixtieth Street in Manhattan, he offered to pay for a ticket to any show I wanted to see for a period of ten months. He called this the Herb Cohen Scholarship. *Lettice and Lovage. Cat on a Hot Tin Roof* with Kathleen Turner. Steppenwolf's production of *The Grapes of Wrath. Aspects of Love.* You'll have a hard time finding a person more versed in the theatrical offerings of New York City, 1990–1991.

Best of all was just wandering around the city with my father, watching him get into discussions with every kind of character on the street. He was like a bear in its natural habitat, a fish returned to its native river. One morning, on the way to breakfast, he was approached by a Hare Krishna who tried to sell him a book called *Forbidden Archeology: The Hidden History of the Human Race.* Herbie was fascinated by the Krishnas, especially their negotiating technique, which he characterized as "the hard sell." In an attempt to gather information, he'd already read the book, which he'd purchased from a Hare Krishna at O'Hare airport. He pulled it from his briefcase as the cultist made his pitch and said, "How about I sell it back?" This offended the Hare Krishna and led to a verbal squabble, though, as mystics, the Krishnas are not supposed to get angry. He waved a finger in Herbie's face; the flower in his hair quivered. He stormed off and found another potential buyer. Herbie appeared at his side as he held up the book and said, "What's he asking? I'll do better." The infuriated Hare Krishna then dropped his price to meet Herbie's, proving, as Herbie claimed he'd meant to from the beginning, that *everyone* negotiates.

We made regular forays to Brooklyn. Herbie would rent a car or flag down an armada of gypsy cabs, directing the fleet like a harbormaster. He made a big deal of it when we exited the Brooklyn–Battery Tunnel or descended the ramp of the Manhattan Bridge into Fort Greene. "Two miles but a light-year away."

Manhattan was glitter and gold, Tiffany and FAO Schwarz, the Plaza, the Pierre, bankers in suits, models in heels. Brooklyn was the old country, the land of our fathers, gangsters, con artists, family men, and *balabustas*. Visiting Betty and Ben meant visiting the house where my mom grew up. Despite all their money, they still lived in middle-class Midwood. The parlor with its flowery wallpaper and cabinet TV, the couches covered in plastic, the china-filled hutch in the dining room.

Ellen tensed up when she stepped through the door. There's no place like your childhood home. She brought presents for her mother and sister, peace offerings—in olden times, she would have sacrificed a goat on the Temple Mount—then went in back to talk. Grandpa Ben would meanwhile load the kids into his car and take us to Cumberland Packing for a tour. Ben referred to the factory, which occupied an entire block at the top of Flushing Avenue, as "the store." The ingenuity of the place, the chutes that delivered the pink packets to the boxes, the belts that carried those boxes to the loading bays, mirrored Ben's mind. It was brilliant, masterful, and cold, saccharine sweet with a bitter aftertaste.

Ellen was always in the front hall when we got back, coat on, waiting to leave. Something had happened. Something had always happened. It could take her a month to recover from one of those visits. She'd go over each detail again and again, trying to remember the exact wording, the exact moment. If she could just figure it out, she'd understand everything. "Sometimes there is nothing to figure out," said Herbie.

Bensonhurst was a relief after Midwood. Herbie's parents were long gone by then, having migrated to Miami Beach with the rest of the Jews, but the streets were the same. The corners and candy stores, the newsstands, bakeries, and pizza parlors, the stairs to the IRT, the shadows beneath the elevated, sparks raining down, kids in club jackets, cigar stores, and delicatessens—just like in the stories. Herbie was a different person in Bensonhurst, profane and free. He rolled down his window as soon as we crossed Sixtieth Street. If he was driving, he'd push back the seat and steer with one hand. He nodded at people as we went by. Now and then, someone shouted his name. He'd shout back. In Bensonhurst, we were seeing my father as he'd been before he was our father, as he still was deep down, when we weren't looking.

He slowed down beside a tough-looking man in a long black coat on one of these trips. Hunched over and walking fast, the man looked as if he didn't want to be seen. He turned and glared, looked in the car, grinned, and said, "Yo, Herbie! When'd you get back?"

No. **34**

THEN CAME THE BAD TIME.

Herbie and Ellen must have known for weeks but had not told me and never would have told me if they could've kept it secret. Same as woodworking and sex, I learned about it at school. I was a freshman at New Trier in Winnetka, Illinois. My brother was at NYU. My sister was in law school in California. I was one of three on paper. In practice, I was an only child.

I was in study hall, talking to a girl named Lucy who said she liked me but not "in that way." She told me two other things that morning. First, that Darth Vader was Luke Skywalker's father. (I was going to see *The Empire Strikes Back* that night.) And second, that my father had been sued for millions of dollars by a writer or writers who claimed that parts of *You Can Negotiate Anything* had been plagiarized. She'd learned this from her mother, who, she said, had heard about it on *Good Morning America*.

When I asked my mother about it after school, she burst into tears.

Though Herbie Cohen is a singular character, built in imitation of no man, these two other writers, authors of less successful books, claimed he had used their stories and ideas. They were asking for a silly amount of money. It was the sort of number you rarely hear outside astronomy class. The fact that two authors had joined to accuse a third of stealing intellectual property seemed self-defeating. If, as they claimed, they'd both had the same material stolen, wouldn't that mean they'd stolen it from each other, too? Herbie was even more confused when he finally got to read the complaint. It was the first time he'd seen such a liberal use of ellipses, with the three little dots connecting clauses that in the text were separated by hundreds of pages, creating new sentences that could possibly be said to read something like their own.

I don't remember the names of the antagonists, or maybe I do, but I'd rather not include them. I will say this: they came from academia, authors, between them, of a basketful of books that had hit without impact, business tomes meant for one section of the store only. Herbie had done something different, new. He'd written a business book that was nominally about business but really about life. It could easily be shelved in Self-Help, Philosophy, or Humor. Which is why it was such a big hit in the business world—because it was not a business book, but a real book, a funny book, a *book* book, the boardroom seen through the eyes of Brooklyn and described in the language of Bensonhurst, less Alfred P. Sloan than Damon Runyon, a street corner kid arguing over the price of an ice cream cone.

It was not just a lawsuit but a culture clash. It was Eighty-Sixth Street and Bay Parkway versus the lecture hall. Whereas the plaintiffs credited themselves with the invention of modern negotiation, Herbie cited the oldest influences known to mankind, Genesis and Exodus, Abraham haggling with Jehovah, Odysseus outsmarting Cyclops, Jesus preaching at Capernaum, the art of give-and-take as depicted by Shakespeare, Dickens, Mel Brooks, Casey Stengel, Mayor Daley, Nikita Khrushchev, Morris Cohen. Many lessons were gleaned from his experience as a claims adjuster, in arms control and hostage negotiation, as a Cohen family court judge, and parent. Because, as he writes, "your real world is a giant negotiating table." He did not claim any ideas as purely his own, or insist they were unique to his book, only that they were true and as truths would have to be included, in some form, in any book about negotiation.

Lyle Stuart urged Herbie to settle the lawsuit. "This happens when you have a hit," he said. "They come out of the woodwork. They know it's cheaper for you to settle than fight. Even if you win, you'll lose. The money. The time. Just pay the bastards."

But Herbie decided to fight. He believed that settling would be like admitting he'd stolen from these people.

"You don't understand publishing," said Stuart.

"I do understand bullies," said Herbie.

Herbie believed appeasing aggression only incites more aggression; the way to deal with a bully, he said, is to hit back quickly and so hard they curse the day they started up with you. "If you hit me, you better kill me," he'd say, "because if you don't kill me, I'm coming back tonight and I'm going to kill you."

According to the plaintiffs, any ideas in common among the three books must have come from them because their books had been published first. But Herbie had been telling his stories to groups and writing them in workbooks since he was a claims adjuster in the early 1960s, meaning, by their own reasoning, any common ideas must have come from Herbie, who accordingly countersued, seeking the same amount they were seeking plus more to compensate for reputational damage and time wasted by frivolous lawsuit.

"With whatever measure you measure, it will be measured to you," said Herbie, quoting the Gospel.

Lyle Stuart scolded Herbie when he found out.

"You're being stupid," he said. "Just pay the ticket and get back in your car."

"You don't understand," said Herbie.

"You're the one who doesn't understand," said Stuart.

"Yeah, well, I guess we understand different," said Herbie.

Grandpa Ben urged Herbie to settle, too. It was a conversation my father would hold against his father-in-law. "Of course, the one time he calls, it's to tell me to quit."

But I'm not sure Ben was wrong. Herbie was confusing his ego with the price of doing business, mistaking a walnut in the batter of life for life itself; he cared too much. If he'd settled, the whole thing would have been forgotten by the end of the year and he would have written a follow-up and the rest of us would have gone on with our lives. But there was no second book, not for decades, nor was there a return to normal life, because the lawsuit became an obsession that seemed to go on forever.

The case progressed slowly; you've never seen anything creep like that. There were depositions in three cities, because one case had been filed in New York, the other in L.A., and the countersuits had been filed in Chicago. Herbie had to pay three sets of attorneys as a result and, in addition to his normal business travel, had to fly from coast to coast to meet with his lawyers, their lawyers, and judges. Legal fees mounted. All the money he'd made on the book had soon been spent defending it. He went into debt. The words he began to use—"Sisyphean," "Kafkaesque," "quixotic"—signaled his desperation.

Ellen, who handled the finances, also told him to settle, but he said, "Never."

"Would you rather go broke?" she asked.

"I'd rather put a gun in my mouth," he answered.

This period felt as if it constituted an age—the Lawsuit age, like the Permian age or the Pleistocene age. Ellen sank first into a mild depression, then into a deep depression. She spent days in her bedroom, not bothering to change out of the blue terry-cloth nightgown she called her shmatta robe. She read drugstore science fiction and watched TV. Herbie did what he'd always done when stressed, the only thing a person in such a situation could do—buried himself in work. Speech after speech. We hardly saw him. If not sitting in New York or L.A. with attorneys, he was at an airport, in a rental car, at a motel, or lecturing a group in a hotel meeting room. If you work yourself to exhaustion, you won't have the strength to worry, he explained.

It took something like five years to resolve the lawsuits, though it felt longer; it felt like my entire childhood. It was the worst time for Herbie, but also the best. He hadn't run when attacked, nor settled. He'd turned and counterattacked. He'd run toward the source of fire. He'd hit back as hard as he could, defying his publisher, father-in-law, and wife. He fought and, in fighting, passed his own test.

When the end finally came, it happened dramatically, in the form of a breakthrough, a surprising turn. The plaintiffs' attorneys hired a private detective to investigate Herbie. He says he's been telling these stories since he worked at Allstate in the 1960s? Well, let's find someone who worked with him back then. If they don't remember him telling those stories, the case falls apart and he'll be forced to settle. The detective did eventually track down one of Herbie's old colleagues, but this man turned out to be the grenade that blows up in the grenade thrower's own hand. Not only did he remember Herbie telling those stories, but he had saved a workbook, written by Herbie in the 1960s, in which many of those stories were included, a primitive version of *You Can Negotiate Anything*. Asked why he'd saved the workbook, the man said, "Because that stuff really works."

The plaintiffs' lawyers tried to bury this man and his testimony, but it all came out in discovery. The witness was deposed by Herbie's lawyers, then questioned by a judge, who flipped through the workbook while looking at *You Can Negotiate Anything*. When the judge accepted the workbook as evidence, the plaintiffs dropped their suit and asked to settle the countersuit. Herbie did not want to settle, but the judge insisted. One defendant paid many thousands of dollars. Ellen had a copy of the check blown up into a poster and hung it on a wall. The other, at Herbie's request, paid into a fund that financed the construction of a bocce court in Brooklyn.

Herbie was still not ready to quit. Outraged by a bill from his L.A. lawyer—"He billed me for the hour he spent eating breakfast!"—he sued his own counsel, which meant another year in court that ended with a refund and a ruling that established case law.

Herbie won in every way a person can win in the system, but at what cost? It consumed years of his life, tortured my mother, and cost him more money than the book itself ever made. When people ask if he won or lost, I say "both." He prevailed, but the process itself became the punishment.

No. **35**

THE EXPERIENCE CHANGED MY FATHER IN A PROFOUND
way; he became addicted to the rush of battle, the feeling that
he was the little guy taking on an evil system. He watched all
his favorite Frank Capra movies—*Mr. Smith Goes to Washington, Mr. Deeds Goes to Town*—with new eyes. He saw himself
as the man from the sticks, forced by fate to stand in the path
of the machine.

When he ran out of battles of his own, he began looking
for those of other people. He became a freelance injustice
fighter. You had to be careful when you told him about your
problems. He might ignore you. Or he might dismiss them as
"nothing," "bullshit," "a walnut in the batter of life." Or he
might become incensed and enraged and involved. In the
end, his involvement might prove a bigger headache than
your original problem. Once Herbie engaged, he was impossible to disengage. The man simply would not quit. You went
to him for sympathy and advice, but wound up in the crew of
crazy captain Ahab.

When a college tried to fire one of my uncles without
cause, my uncle, who'd been a professor at the school for decades, called Herbie, who at first did not care, then, when he
focused on the details, became engaged. *What makes them
think they can treat a person like that?* I don't know all the details, but, suffice it to say, my uncle attended one meeting
wearing a "wire," then a phone call was surreptitiously recorded,
then Herbie turned up at a meeting of the administration
unexpectedly and with great flair, in the way of Wyatt Earp or
Batman. My uncle was reinstated with full pay, though he did

agree to take a cut in the dental portion of his health-care plan.

When a local TV executive attempted to fire Herbie's friend Joan without cause—Joan drew the balls for the daily lotto—the headman, who'd wanted to replace Joan with a relative, found himself across a desk from crazy captain Ahab. Herbie, having dissected Joan's contract like a Talmudist, got her back on the air by "hanging the bastards with their own words."

He hated when one of his kids got in trouble at school, but loved it, too, because it gave him a chance to battle injustice. That is, if he felt we were in the right. If we were in the wrong, we deserved what we got, but if we were getting screwed, then here comes Captain Ahab with a harpoon in his hand.

I was getting a D in sophomore English. Herbie, who had not been paying attention, noticed one of my marked-up assignments while eating ice cream late at night. He became infuriated as he read through it. "Of course he's getting a D," he told my mother. "The question makes no sense. This person, who cannot write, is grading our son's writing."

He believed the questions were riddled with prejudice. In one, which was about "conventional wisdom," she gave, as an example of "conventional wisdom," the belief that "Jews are stingy" or "Mexicans are lazy."

"That's not conventional wisdom," said Herbie. "It's slander."

He made an appointment with the teacher, then sat across the desk in her office at New Trier. My mother was at the meeting, and so was I. The teacher, who was curt and officious, showed my father one of my papers—D—then began going through it line by line, explaining every deficiency in my work. Herbie asked if he could see the assignment sheet she'd handed out for the exam. He read it as she talked, took a red pencil out of his pocket, and began marking it up. He handed it back with a grade: D. Before he could finish explaining why she had done so poorly, and why a poorly phrased question will result in a confused essay, she started furiously quoting her credentials.

She said, "I have been teaching students for fifteen years."

He said, "I have been teaching students for thirty years."

She said, "I attended the University of Illinois."

He said, "I attended Yale."

She said, "I have a master's from the Columbia Teachers College."

He said, "I have a PhD from Caltech."

My mother turned to me and said, "Richard, go back to class."

"But I—"

"*Go to class!*"

Later, when I told my father I was afraid to go back into that teacher's classroom—"she's definitely going to fail me now"—he said, "No, she's not. She's going to treat you very well. And you'll get a B in that class."

That is what happened.

That was sophomore year. Senior year, I had a dustup with a teacher who'd been driven mad by noise in the hallway. He was a tall, dour, long-faced Latin instructor who insisted that his students call him Professor. One day, I made the mistake of shouting to a friend in the hall outside his classroom. He said something to me through the window of the closed door.

I laughed nervously, then said, "I can't hear you." He came running out, grabbed me by the shoulders, and shoved me into the lockers. I raised my hands in a gesture of surrender. He said he was taking me to see the adviser chairman, the top cop for each grade. I refused, and said I was taking him to see the principal, who outranked the adviser chairman. He followed me to the office, where I asked the secretary if I could see Mr. McGee. He was out. I left my name and explained the issue. "Okay," said the Professor. "Now we're going to see the adviser chairman."

The school day was over, so I said, "No. Now I'm going home."

The next morning, when I showed up for my first class, the teacher, said, "I'm not even allowed to let you sit down. You have to go directly to the adviser chairman."

The adviser chairman wore tight plaid pants and wire-frame glasses. He did not let me explain, but merely told me I'd been suspended for a week and had to leave school grounds immediately. I called the house from the pay phone, expecting my mother to answer. I needed a ride. Herbie picked up instead. When I explained what had happened, he said, "I'm coming down there."

The adviser chairman would not let him talk either: "The boy is suspended; that's the end of it." At some point, after he'd cut Herbie off for the fifth or sixth time, Herbie looked at the ceiling behind the man's desk. This silenced the adviser chairman, who turned, had a look for himself, then asked, "Where are you looking?"

"Over your head," said Herbie. "Because that's where I'm going."

The day ended in the principal's office, where Herbie, Ellen, and I sat with the adviser chairman and the Professor, who, in his fantastical version, said I'd been making noise in the hall, then looked through the window into his class, laughed, and said, "I'm laughing at you."

"That insolence is what made me lose my temper," he said.

I denied all of this. It was crazy. The conversation went on. Herbie stood up and asked to be directed to the bathroom. He was gone for five minutes, then appeared outside the closed door. He was saying something through the window. Then he came in, sat down, and said, "And if we agree to that, I think we can all go home."

"Agree to what?" asked the principal.

"To what I just said," said Herbie.

"I couldn't hear you," said the principal.

"Aha!" Herbie shouted, standing and pointing with a Perry Mason flourish. "So if you could not hear me, how could the Professor have possibly heard Richard through the same kind of closed door in a hallway crowded with students?"

There was no suspension. I agreed to steer clear of the Professor's hallway, he apologized for pushing me into the lockers, and as my father had predicted, we all went home.

No. 36

THE BIGGEST OF THESE FIGHTS CAME DURING MY SENIOR year at Tulane University. For me, it's like a Bible story. I've analyzed it again and again over the years, searching for message and meaning. As I've said, Herbie occasionally taught by counterexample. By watching him, you could learn what *not* to do, which is get overly involved, invested, or entangled with the offal of the world.

It's funny. He built his book around a philosophy, which he boiled down to a gleaming phrase—"the key to life is to care, but not *that* much"—but even a cursory study of his behavior will show a man in a constant state of over-caring. *You Can Negotiate Anything* was a self-help book, and as anyone who has spent time around the authors of such books can tell you, those who write self-help are those most in need of self-help. Their work is a literary version of whistling past the graveyard, talking to themselves in the dark. Herbie's favorite aphorism defines his behavior more accurately than anything he's ever said about caring: "If you're walking on thin ice, you might as well dance."

I was at home on winter break, telling anyone who would listen about my college creative writing class, which had been my first experience with a cult of personality. The professor was a campus god, the closest thing the school had to a resident genius. His name was not Kenneth Schlichter, but that's what I'll call him here. His beard grew long beneath his chin, but his cheeks were smooth, an antiquated hairstyle that gave him the aura of an old-time transcendentalist. His eyes were small and hard; his demeanor arrogant and mean. He handled students as if handling creepy crawlies. When I complained to another professor about how the class was run—you'd sit at a table with ten other students, read your story, which first Schlichter, then everyone else, as if on cue, tore to pieces—he defended the professor, saying, "Kenneth Schlichter is an artist with a particular pedagogical style: he says he has not done his job properly if he hasn't left blood on the floor."

I had trouble with Schlichter from the start. I had a different taste in writing, for one, a different idea of what makes a good story. Taking this as a sign of disrespect—*So I didn't love Ann Beattie, so what?*—he developed a keen dislike for me. I felt it when my turn came to read my work to the class. He ripped into every story but went after mine with a special gusto, an undisguised glee. I sat through the general pummeling that followed without protest or complaint, because that's what you were supposed to do. I knew using my story as the occasion to make a general complaint about the professor's method would seem like sour grapes. Nobody likes a whiner. So I waited. I waited in the way of an advocate who waits for the perfect test case to bring to the Supreme Court, the case that will demonstrate the fallacy of the entire system.

In the meantime, I refused to take part in the weekly table read beatdown. I absented myself, which did not go unnoticed. I recited the first graph of a Camus essay we'd been reading in Philosophy to myself as I sat glowering: "What is a rebel? A man who says no, but whose refusal does not imply a renunciation. He is also a man who says yes, from the moment he makes his first gesture of rebellion. A slave who has taken orders all his life suddenly decides that he cannot obey some new command."

The test case came as a story about the art of pool hustling written by a girl in class. She did not want to be a writer. I knew this because we were friends in what I'd taken to calling every place that was not Kenneth Schlichter's workshop: "the outside." She was a business major who'd enrolled in the class in the spirit of self-actualization, growth. She was the carefree amateur who, on a dare, takes the stage during open mic night at Dangerfield's.

Schlichter lit into the story as soon as she'd read the last sentence—"and the girl slept the righteous sleep of the hustler who knows she will never have to play the game again." The fact that it had been a good story, better, in my opinion, than many of those *New Yorker* and *Paris Review* stories we had to read for class, was just another occasion for Schlichter to pick up his favorite terms, which he wielded like hammers. "Cliché." "Trite." "Sophomoric." The conch shell then went around the table, with each student, the good along with the bad, joining in. It was like something you'd see outside a bar at three in the morning, drunks in a circle, kicking some poor bastard to a pulp.

"What is a rebel?" I asked myself, when the spotlight fell on me. I defended the story briefly, then went after the nature of the class itself. "The professor and his methods are unsound." It was an uprising and, as such, attracted a handful of followers. You could almost hear the groan of cracking ice. Spring was in the air, regicide.

Schlichter looked at his watch, threw up his hands, and called for a fifteen-minute break. The girl who'd read the story gathered up her business text and copy of *Granta* and ran out. I hung back to talk to Schlichter. He was furious. "If you don't like how I teach my class, you are free to drop," he said.

"What are you even doing in here?" I asked.

"I am teaching my students how to become writers."

"She left in tears," I said.

"The truth hurts," he said.

"She doesn't even want to be a writer," I said. "She's a business major. And now, because of this, she'll never do another creative thing."

"If that's the case, then she shouldn't be in my class."

A few weeks later, when my next turn came around, I read a poem I'd written about the professor. It was coded but clear, and I read it only because a friend said I'd never have the guts. It was called "The Unique Cliché" and it ended with the following stanza:

Fuck you
you fuck
Fuck you

Schlichter did not criticize my poem—he said only, "That's not poetry"—but instead ended class early, then refused to interact with me for the rest of the semester. As if I were invisible. As if I had died. He skipped my turn in the circle, and never let me comment. Whenever I handed in an assignment, it was back in my mailbox moments later, unread and always given the same grade: B. This was smart. How do you complain about a B? But it was not the grade that bothered me; it was the lack of interaction. I wanted to be read. Schlichter knew that, so that's what he would not give me.

We were required to write a long story for the final, almost a novella. I spent months on it, assuming, because this would mark the end of our relationship, he'd cast aside his feelings and read my work. *Wrong.* It was in my mailbox ten minutes after I'd turned it in. Grade? B. I went to his office; he refused to see me. I met the chairman of the English Department, who listened with sympathy, then promised to talk to Professor Schlichter. He called the next day and told me to resubmit my story. "He'll take another look," he promised.

Once again, it was back in my mailbox ten minutes after I'd turned it in. The original B had been crossed out and replaced by an even bigger B. The department chair got angry when I went to see him again. "What do you want?" he demanded. "This man, this literary man, has given you a better than passing grade. Be happy."

I told my mother, brother, sister, and friend Jamie the story over winter break, but none of them cared. "My parents are getting divorced and you're bitching about a B?" Jamie asked. I tried to tell Herbie what had happened, but couldn't get his attention. He was busy with other things. Finally, near the end of break, he sighed and said, "If I sit down and listen, will you finally shut up about this?"

"Yes."

As I told the story, I could see by his posture and the look in his eyes that I'd gotten more than his attention. He started out apathetic, then became curious. By the time I'd finished, he was enraged. When he asked, "Did that bastard really say he likes to leave blood on the floor?" I knew I'd inadvertently summoned Captain Ahab.

He fired off the first angry letter before I was even back at school. By the end of the semester, dozens of complaints, explanations, and suggestions of redress had gone back and forth between Herb Cohen, the chairman of the Tulane English Department, the dean of the school of arts and sciences, and finally the university president. I still have the carbon copies. "Kafkaesque," "quixotic," "ignoble"—the letters are riddled with the words Herbie used whenever grappling with what he considered the machine. He wanted more than promises. He wanted action. The professor must be removed.

The girl who'd been driven from class must be apologized to. The school must examine the method used in its workshops. When these demands were denied, he added others. The chairman of the department must be replaced. Every student in the class, with the exception of his own son, must have his or her grade retroactively changed to an A. Conference calls followed, proposals and counterproposals, all of which, because Herbie kept me out of the loop, I was oblivious to. I assumed he'd dropped the matter when I started the second semester of my senior year. I'd stopped caring about Kenneth Schlichter. If I didn't care, why should he?

I was shocked when I spotted Herbie standing under the big moss-covered oak tree outside the administration building that spring, a thousand miles from where he was supposed to be.

"What are you doing here?" I asked.

"I have a meeting with the president, the dean, and that professor."

I got confused, then irritated, then angry.

"It's over," I said.

"Not for me."

"What do you even want?"

"It's all in the memo."

"This is crazy."

"I'm not doing it for you," he said. "I'm doing for the next kid."

Years later, long after I'd graduated and joined the workforce, I called Glencoe looking for my father.

"He's not here," said my mother.

"Where is he?"

"New Orleans."

"Why?"

"He's meeting with the president of Tulane."

"About what?"

"What do you think?"

"No!"

It made no sense to me. I begged him to stop. He said he would not stop until he had achieved his goals. In the end, the department chairman was removed or maybe just stepped down—five years had gone by—and a letter had been placed in Kenneth Schlichter's file. In other words, he'd achieved nothing.

But that's not how he saw it.

"You are forgetting about the difference between the *what*

and the *how*," he told me. "The *what* might seem like nothing, but this case was all about the *how*—that being me getting on them, and staying on them, and acting like a lunatic."

"The next time that professor is about to destroy some poor kid," he explained, "he'll stop himself because he'll be thinking, 'Maybe this one has a crazy father, too.'"

No. 37

HERBIE'S PARENTS HAD FOLLOWED THE SIREN SONG TO Miami Beach, which Grandpa Morris called "the true promised land of the Jews." Morris and Esther lived in a one-bedroom condo in North Miami Beach, where the streets are numbered in triple digits and the condo complexes have elaborate names. Theirs was called the Three Seasons, because there is no winter in Florida. It had a kidney-shaped pool, a canasta room, and a superannuated exercise center where a big canvas strap shook you up like prunes in a blender set to chop. There was a half dome of wooden rollers with a function I was never able to ascertain, as well as medicine balls, dumbbells, and the kind of exercise bike that, when you ride it, pushes your knees up above your ears.

The Three Seasons was populated by Polish- and Russian-born Jews who'd reached Miami Beach after long lives in New York. To us, they seemed ancient, but in the 1950s and 1960s, when most of them made the move, they were middle-aged. The stent, the bypass, the pacemaker, and statin have emptied out the acacia-shaded halls of the subtropical South. Morris, who'd spent his early years across the sea, never stopped marveling at Florida's abundance. For him, the most beautiful phrase in English was "Fresh squeezed."

Political arguments and feuds that had seemingly been left behind in Brooklyn were picked back up in the condo complexes along Collins Avenue. These people had seen a lot and known a lot and done a lot and loved a lot and, though still vibrant, had been forced into indolence in this Candy Land with nothing but sunshine, palm trees, and swimming pools.

What else were they going to do but bicker and talk about their grandchildren?

Esther was a poolside big shot. From a certain point of view, she could have been called a bully. Even if you'd known her all your life, it was impossible to tell if she was *trying* to be mean. It just happened, in the way of a natural phenomenon. She said whatever came into her mind without consideration, and as a result people's feelings got hurt. Once, confronting a neighbor whose standoffishness confused her, Esther asked, "Why do you hate me, Fatso?"

No. 38

MORRIS HAD SUFFERED VARIOUS AILMENTS OVER THE years. In October 1972, when some of his symptoms became acute, he checked himself into a hospital. Doctors found a mass in his stomach. The word "cancer" exploded in the room. Surgery was scheduled.

Herbie sat alone with his father the night before the operation.

Morris put a hand—he had warm fleshy hands—on top of

Herbie's and asked his son to judge his life. "Have I been a good father? Have I been a good man?"

"Yes, Pop. You've done great."

Morris died in his sleep early the next morning, before the doctors could operate. Herbie believes Morris died because he wanted to die. "He knew what the next few years would be like, and didn't want it," Herbie told me.

As I've said, Morris served as a circuit breaker for Esther. He stopped the current when she crossed the line, went too far, said what might be thought but should not be voiced. Laying his fingers on her wrist, he'd whisper, "Enough, Esther. Enough." She had no breaker after Morris was gone. She'd just go on and on, ripping and roaring, offending, infuriating, and scandalizing. She did it in person and did it on the phone. Picking up the receiver between 7:00 and 9:00 p.m.— Grandma Esther's witching hours—was like playing Russian roulette. You'd probably be okay. When my sister's live-in boyfriend answered, Esther told him that he was living in sin and should expect a visit from "the Malamoufitz," the angel of death. Once, when Herbie picked up, Esther said, "What happened? You used to be good-looking."

She did not wait for a person on the other end to answer, but spoke before you had time to say hello, demanding, "Who's dat?" Even if she dialed your number by accident, she was ready to pivot and blast. Once, after I'd answered her first question, "Who's dat?" she said, "I meant to call your cousin Robbie, but, since I have you, what's this your parents tell me about you dating a girl with the sugar diabetes? If a thing like that gets into the gene pool, it stays there a thousand years."

Many nights ended with the sound of Herbie talking to his mother, a kind of 1062 Bluff Road theme song that ran beneath the action like sitcom music: "Ma! Ma! Ma! No, Ma! Why, Ma! Yes, Ma! Oh, Ma! Ma! Ma! Ma!"

Esther got worse with age. She said hurtful things to people who simply wanted to sit by the kidney-shaped pool and read. That's why Herbie was not unhappy when she took up with Izzy Greenspun, another Polish-born Jew circum-navigating his golden years. Herbie hoped Izzy would do the job of circuit breaker, calm Esther, dull the sharp edge. But that's not what happened.

Izzy lived most of the year in Skokie, Illinois, then home to the world's largest concentration of Holocaust survivors. Once, when I was searching for his number, my brother said, "Look in the white pages. How many Izzy Greenspuns can there be in Skokie?"

The answer was a lot.

Izzy met Esther while visiting a friend with a condo in the Three Seasons. Esther was eighty-two. Izzy said he was eighty-five. He began making trips to see her in Florida. She stayed at his house in Skokie. That's where I first met him. I was twelve. A kid usually can't tell what an old person had been like when that old person had been young. Age obscures. That was not the case with Izzy. As soon as I'd spent five min-utes with this white-haired little dandy, I knew that he was and always had been a nebbish.

He wore powder-blue pants hitched to his chest, white shoes, a white belt with a silver buckle, a short-sleeved button-down shirt, the breast pocket weighted with pencils, reading glasses, and a calculator for determining tips. He did not enunciate. If he'd been a gangster, they would have called him Mumbles. You could never tell if he was speaking English or Yiddish. Once upon a time, he sold shoes at Carson Pirie Scott, a Chicago department store. He was a retired shoe salesman, a widower with two grown daughters. There was Dolores, whom my brother Steven called Dolo. She was a Chicago public school teacher in polyester pants and heavy makeup, hair worn in a towering beehive, lips puckered for the sort of kiss that leaves a lavender stamp. And there was Helen, whom my brother called Lady Death because she claimed she'd seen Death walking across our yard. Steven spoke of the family as if it were an accounting firm, saying, "Izzy, Dolo & Lady Death."

Izzy was considered a catch in Miami Beach. He was un-attached, was fully ambulatory, and could drive at night. When Herbie looked at Izzy, he saw everything his father Morris was not—cloying, obtuse, and clueless, a man who, rather than moderate Esther's excesses, fed them like acceler-ant. Whatever she said, Izzy repeated in a stammering Yid-dish accent—a grim echo. If she said, "President Carter is a bum," he said, "Listen to Grandmommy. Grandmommy knows. Grandmommy says President Carter is a bum." If she said, "Anwar Sadat is a gonif. I wouldn't trust him any farther than I could throw him," he said, "Listen to Grandmommy. Grandmommy knows. Grandmommy says Anwar Sadat is a gonif. She wouldn't throw him."

The relationship developed quickly; that's what happens when a couple's combined age is 167. Izzy began spending winters at the condo in Miami Beach. Esther began spend-ing summers in Izzy's bungalow in Skokie. You could safely drink red wine in any room of that house, because everything was covered in plastic. A plastic trail that started at the front door, crossed the shag-carpeted living room, skirted the plastic-sheathed couch and plastic-coated La-Z-Boy, before ending at the kitchen, where Izzy was amplifying Esther on the subject of Middle East peace. "Listen to Grandmommy. Grandmommy knows. Grandmommy says the man is a *shtarker*."

Izzy and Esther were married one June morning in the mid-1980s. There was a ceremony at a synagogue in Skokie followed by a catered lunch. The limo that carried my family to the event stopped on the way to drop me off at the bus that would take me to camp. Herbie put his arm around me as we crossed the parking lot, saying, "So what? You'll miss the wedding. I'm sure you'll be back for the funeral."

It was not a great day for Herbie. In the early afternoon, Esther said, "If I'd met Izzy before I met Morris, I wouldn't have given Morris a second look." In the late afternoon, it rained.

During Christmas break, my mother put me on a plane to Miami to visit "Grandma and her husband." Esther and Izzy shared a "Hollywood double," twin beds pushed together and made up with a single sheet. *Do they have sex?* was the big question. When I asked my mother, she changed the subject. When I asked my sister, she said, "Yes they do."

We spent the afternoons on the pool deck, sailing through the hours with a gaggle of other ancient Jews. Esther was deeply involved in condo politics, a master of the canasta room filibuster. A picture of her group—they're awaiting the results of a vote they know they have in the bag—shows

Esther as she was in the decades after Morris, less yenta than mob boss, ward heeler, stone-cold political killer, and bagman, the big stick and driving wheel. She was Sam Giancana sharing a laugh with Bugsy Siegel. She was Hyman Roth sitting with Michael Corleone in Havana, saying, "Michael, we're bigger than U.S. Steel."

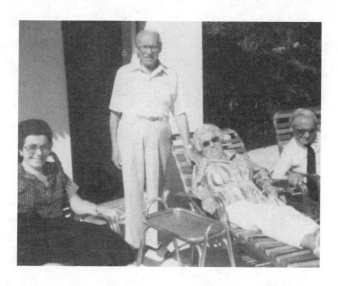

Izzy said he was eighty-five when he met Esther, which was a lie. He was closer to a hundred. She did not find out until she looked at his death certificate: Isidore Greenspun, born Motal, Poland, 1885; died Miami Beach, Florida 1983. That line is the story of the American Jews in microcosm.

Izzy went unexpectedly. The way Esther told the story, it was impossible to know if she was joking. "Izzy was doing the dishes," she said. "I was in the bathroom. I heard a crash. I

thought Izzy dropped a dish. It turned out what Izzy dropped was dead."

Izzy's body was flown to Chicago for burial. It was my first funeral. Esther did not seem terribly upset. She cared, but not *that* much. She began to forget Izzy as soon as he was in the ground. In the last years of her life, she did not even remember Izzy. If asked about him, she'd look at you quizzically. On the buzzer of her condo, she was identified as "Mrs. Morris Cohen." It was my brother who found the perfect words for the relationship: "Izzy come. Izzy go."

When Esther turned ninety, Herbie and his sister, Renee, hired a nurse to help out around the condo. Esther's body was strong—she was built like Mary Lou Retton—but her mind had started to slip. And she was lonely. Herbie enrolled her in a summer camp for seniors, where campers stayed in a grand old boardwalk hotel in Long Beach, Long Island. Every public space of the hotel had been painted a single color. There was a red room, a blue room, a yellow room. Steven still speaks of the "tragic beauty of the green room."

Check-in was filled with Esther's contemporaries, nonagenarians who'd been born in Europe before the Flood. Herbie bumped into a long-lost relative in the lobby, Aunt Helen, the "war bride" who met and married his uncle Nathan in Paris after the armistice. Herbie had not seen Helen since Nathan's funeral, decades before. Escorting her carefully across the floor, Herbie said, "Hey, Ma! Look who I found."

Esther gave Helen, whom she had not seen in thirty years, the once-over, then said, "That slut?" and turned away.

Esther did not make it to a hundred, but got close. For a time, she was one of the only living Americans born in the first decade of the twentieth century. With her generation, an entire sensibility—tough-minded, sarcastic, strong—exited the world. She suffered dementia at the end. She deteriorated in phases. At first, she'd get trapped in a detailed memory. For a time, she believed every day was January 3, 1974. She had just taken me to see a Jerry Lewis double feature. I was five. She bought me a sandwich. I dropped it. She bought me another sandwich, and I dropped that one, too! Cousins whom I had not heard from in years would call and say, "I've just been to see Grandma. Wow, is she mad at you!"

Then she spoke only of death, of being ready to die, of impatiently waiting to die. She said the Malamoufitz had lost her address. "He must have stopped at a party, had a few drinks, put it down on a counter, and lost it." Then she could not remember what day or time or year it was, or even what country she was in. At the end, her mind settled on a single phrase, which she repeated: "I'm scared. I'm scared. I'm scared." It was awful, and you wanted to help, but how? Everyone said this did not mean she really was scared, only that her mind had become stuck on these words, that it was like a mantra and might have been anything, but I'm not so sure. She really did seem scared. At one point, while she was sitting with my father—she'd been asking for Herbie; he'd been saying, "I'm here, Ma"—her mind seemed to clear. She stared at him for a moment, then said, "Do you mean to tell me that *you* are the original Herbie?"

It almost came as a relief when the Malamoufitz finally found her condo. Endings are sad because most lives seem only partially lived. You always have a feeling there was still more flavor in that gum. That was not the case with Esther. She got every bit of taste out of her piece.

My brother spoke at the funeral, as did my cousin David, Esther's oldest grandchild. David is a well-known cardiologist. His words were beautiful, but I kept thinking of something Esther once asked him: "If you're such a brilliant doctor, why are you bald?"

Esther was buried in a family plot on Staten Island. The gate was locked when we arrived. We had to call the caretaker. He apologized as he ran up, saying, "There's been vandalism, swastikas and broken headstones."

We drove in a caravan down narrow, weed-choked cemetery lanes. The plots had all been filled, the grounds allowed to dilapidate. Esther would be the last person buried there.

Morris's father, Noah, the patriarch, was in the center of the plot, his stone higher than the others. A fresh hole was waiting for Esther, dirt piled beside it. She'd spend eternity beside Morris, who'd already been here for more than twenty years. As the coffin was lowered, my sister poked me and whispered, "My God, they're burying her next to Helen the Slut."

We stood in line by the grave, each waiting to throw in a spade of dirt. Before he tossed in the first shovelful, Herbie looked down at the coffin and said, "Here you go, Ma."

We stopped at a diner on the way back to the city. Herbie was quiet. We talked as if he were not there.

"I'm an orphan," he finally said.

"No you're not," said my brother. "David Copperfield was an orphan. Arnold from *Diff'rent Strokes* was an orphan. You're sixty-five years old. How can you be a sixty-five-year-old orphan?"

"It doesn't matter how old you are," said Herbie. "When your parents die, you're an orphan."

"Then everyone becomes an orphan," said my brother.

"That's right," said Herbie. "Everyone does become an orphan."

No. 39

THE DEATHS OF HIS PARENTS DID NOT CHANGE HERBIE'S personality, but they did change his sense of time. He seemed to know his days were numbered and intended to use them to prepare his children. His words became portentous and profound as his mother aged toward senescence. Every phrase seemed to take on a second, deeper meaning. He took renewed interest in the various projects of my life, from the serious to the inane.

As for the inane, take the example of the North Shore Screen Doors, the twelve-inch softball team I captained in the Glencoe Summer League during my college years. We played on a dirt field under stadium lights on Wednesdays and Saturdays. We won the championship that first season. The next season, some of our best players, having gained weight and lost motivation while away at school, seemingly forgot how to play. It was demoralizing. We couldn't win a game.

Several teammates came to me in the way of an intervention. They wanted me to ask Herbie to take over as coach, because they loved being around him, because they thought he looked like Walter Matthau in *The Bad News Bears*, because they believed he could help.

I asked my father, assuming he'd say no. He'd taken a big advance from a publisher and was working like mad to finish his second book. Ellen had moved him to my old bedroom, which had been turned into an office. She connected the lights to timers. They went on automatically when he was supposed to start working and went off automatically when he was supposed to stop. From down the hall, I could hear the click, followed by Herbie, who, having been plunged into darkness, shouted, "Goddamnit! I'm a grown man!" But he was having trouble with the second book, so was looking for any sort of diversion. I'd approached him at a time of restlessness, boredom, and anxiety, always a dangerous moment to be in his vicinity, because that's when Herbie sets off on quests.

When he said yes, I expected him to be a big-picture manager, interested less in batting orders and lineups than in atmosphere and wisdom. I was wrong. He spent a week watching us play, then scouted every other team in the league. Ellen was furious. The lights switched on and off, but the office was empty. When she confronted him—"When are you going to finish your book?"—he said, "Ninety-nine percent of deals close within an hour of the deadline." When she protested— "You've already missed the deadline"—he said, "Then it wasn't really the deadline, was it?"

Herbie asserted control in the second week, shuffling the batting order, moving the players to new positions, and recruiting ringers. Most astonishingly, he devised eccentric defensive shifts, a unique arrangement for each hitter in the league. On some plays, he deployed a single infielder and put the rest of us in the outfield. If a ground ball hitter was at the plate, he did the opposite, leaving the center fielder in place but moving everyone else into the infield. As in Germany, he was trying to beat the superior with the inferior. Game theory.

It worked, and we began winning, but I hated it. This was decades before such shifts became common MLB practice, and to my eye it looked silly and made us into a laughing-stock. When I complained, he said, "They can laugh and we can win. To me, that's a good trade."

During what turned out to be our last game of the season—he'd gotten us into the playoffs—our argument went public. We stood on the pitcher's mound during a time-out yelling at each other as what felt like the entire town watched. The bases were loaded. We were up by one. He wanted to intentionally walk the hitter—no one gets intentionally walked in softball—giving up the tying run but avoiding a batter he was convinced—based on scouting—would kill us.

When I refused, he ordered me off the field—I was play-ing catcher—and called for my friend Dennis, who'd never been in a single game, to replace me. I refused. Herbie cursed. I cursed back. He shouted at me. Then I said, "That's it! You're fired."

He stopped, stared at me, looked at the team, looked at the people in the bleachers, shook his head sadly, then walked away. The crowd booed. I told our pitcher to go ahead and "pitch the goddamn ball," resulting in the longest twelve-inch home run I've ever seen. The ball climbed above the lights and vanished into the dark.

No. 40

AS FOR THE IMPORTANT, TAKE MY GRAD SCHOOL AP-plications.

I was a senior in college. When Herbie asked what I planned to do after graduation, I told him I hoped to get a job at a newspaper or magazine. I wanted to be a writer.

"If you really want to be a writer," he said, "you should go to law school. That way, if it doesn't work out, you'll have something to fall back on."

I told him I did not want something to fall back on be-cause people who have something to fall back on usually end up "falling back on it."

We fought about this for months. He'd get mad, throw up his hands, and say, "If you know so much, do it your way. Don't listen to me. What do I know? I'm only twice your age. Just don't come back to me when you need help."

Over time, the law school debate took on symbolic importance in my mind. I was fighting to make my own decisions and live my own life. I felt a tremendous sense of accomplishment when he finally backed off. It was not the bar mitzvah that made me a man, but this: I had battled the old man and won. The future stood before me like a great empty road.

Several weeks later, I began receiving skinny envelopes in the mail, rejection letters from law and graduate schools I'd never applied to. Herbie had filled out the paper work, written the essays, and applied in my name. Some of his choices struck me as ridiculous. Caltech? MIT? I'd only taken a single math class in college, and it was called the Fundamentals of Arithmetic.

"How did you ever think I could get into Caltech or MIT?" I asked him.

"The kids at these schools are the smartest math and science kids in the world," he said. "Not just in the country, but the world. Everywhere they've been, they've been the smartest in these subjects. Now, for the first time, they're going to be around kids who are just as smart or smarter, and it's going to make them uncomfortable. They're going to need different kinds of people around, people with a different kind of intelligence—creative people. I thought maybe that could be you. At Caltech," he explained, "you'd be like the nose that can hear."

I received twenty-five rejections that spring, and one acceptance. When I complained about the humiliation, Herbie said, "I've done you a favor, kid. You want to be a writer? Well, the toughest thing a writer has to deal with is rejection. Learning to ignore it and move on. I've prepared you for the future."

No. 41

IF YOU ASKED HERBIE ABOUT HIS HEALTH, HE'D ANSWER
with one word: "Perfect." If you asked about his blood pressure, cholesterol, blood sugar, he'd say, "Low," "Good," "Fine."
None of which was true. The fact is, Herbie Cohen is man as
preexisting condition.

By the time he sold the Glencoe house in 1996, he was
either treating or keeping an eye on a dozen maladies, including type 2 diabetes, chronic migraine, bad back. He was
accident-prone. He was reckless behind the wheel. He took
dumb chances. He dozed off and hit a tree, sliced his finger
while cutting a bagel, fell off a chairlift while telling a story.
He responded to each injury the way he believed a man is
supposed to respond. He ignored it. Quoting Groucho Marx,
he'd say, "Never complain, never explain." He valued one
quality above all others: the ability to work while hurt. He
bragged about his pain threshold. Here was a man who fell
asleep in the dentist's chair during a root canal. If asked while
lying in a ditch shot full of holes how he was doing, he'd say,
"Fine, and you?" No matter what ailed him, he denied it. He'd
never tell you what the doctor really said. According to him,
every bill of health was a clean bill of health, every test negative. When I told him I was worried about him—no one
could behave the way he behaved and last—he said what he
always said: "Nothing can kill me."

When he did have a close call—this happened with
frequency—he'd focus not on the risk he'd taken but on the
miracle of his survival. "If that didn't kill me," he'd say, after
retaking control of the car, regaining consciousness in the

hospital, or wrapping a tourniquet around his knee, "nothing will."

He was a firm believer in ignoring symptoms, whether they be chest pains, a mysteriously swollen ankle, a lump on his neck. "If you ignore these things," he said, "they tend to go away." When it came to medical care, he had a paramount rule: avoid unnecessary surgery. "The hospital is the most dangerous place in the world," he explained. "That's where they kill you."

It's an ideology that nearly ended his life in 1992. At age fifty-nine, his heart began sending up flares. It started as dizziness. He felt shaky walking up hills. It did not even have to be a steep hill or a long hill. Any hill. Even the kind you're not 100 percent sure is a hill. The world reeled when he reached the top. Little things looked big. Close things looked distant. There was sweat above his lip. He put his hands on his knees and stared at the ground, breathing hard, waiting for the landscape to settle.

Ellen: "What is it?"

Herbie: "Nothing."

Ellen: "What are you going to do about it?"

Herbie: "Nothing."

Herbie and Ellen were spending part of the year in Miami Beach, not in old Jewish North Miami Beach, but in booming Art Deco South Beach, where they'd bought an apartment. The sidewalk climbed as it went from the front door to Herbie's favorite coffee shop, and it was in the course of that climb, as he went for his skim cappuccino and *New York Times*, that he was overcome by the light-headedness that got worse by the day. Though he always answered Ellen's worried questions in the same dismissive way—"It's nothing. I'm fine"—he must've known.

He had to sit down on the curb to catch his breath one morning. On another, as he was sitting down to catch his breath, his eyes rolled back and he slumped on the green spiky grass. Ellen was dialing 911 when he opened his eyes and closed her phone, saying, "Don't. I'm fine."

Ellen: "You're not fine!"

Herbie: "I am fine. I promise."

He believed the source of his trouble was not his heart but his weight. If he lost twenty-five pounds, he said, he'd be good. "Give me two months to get in shape," he told Ellen. "That's all I ask. After that, if I don't have this fixed, I'll go see a doctor."

Ellen agreed on one condition: he could run on a treadmill at the gym, ride a stationary bike, use Nautilus machines, but he was not to put one foot on a StairMaster, which, as a result of a segment on *CBS Sunday Morning*, she thought of as "the widow maker." As in a dream, she could see him slumped on its steps, sweat covered, dead. Herbie assented. No StairMaster.

His symptoms worsened even as the weight came off. On more than one occasion, he was taken by ambulance to the nearest hospital. Each time, when he regained his senses, he'd check himself out and return to his routine. His behavior was always backed by reason. He said he checked himself out of Mount Sinai Medical Center on Alton Road because "the doctors looked like bums." He said he checked himself out of Coral Gables Hospital because his admission was based on a misunderstanding. "I wasn't unconscious when you called the paramedics," he told Ellen. "I was resting." He said he checked himself out of Miami General because it was Christmas Day and the nurse rolled a ham into the cardiac unit and was serving slices to patients, and "What kind of hospital serves ham to heart patients?"

He went back on the road for work in the spring, which greatly expanded his range of hospital admission. By May, he'd been in and out of emergency rooms across the country. Later, when we learned of this—as per Herbie's insistence, Ellen wasn't talking—I suggested he write a *Zagat* guide to emergency rooms, an idea he did not appreciate. Meanwhile, he'd dropped fifty pounds via fasting and spartan workout. Though he believed he was making himself healthy, he was in fact summoning the very emergency he was working so hard to avoid. Irony. He was down to 165 pounds by July. He called it his "fighting weight"; it was more like his "dying weight."

I had a job in Manhattan that summer. I got the message from my sister when I returned from lunch. It was marked "Urgent." I'd never seen that box checked before.

Sharon was calm when I got her on the phone, but I could hear my mother crying in the background. Herbie had collapsed at the Watergate gym in Washington, D.C., where my parents lived part of the year. A trainer, having seen him go down, called an ambulance. He'd been admitted to George Washington University Hospital. "It's bad," Sharon told me. "Someone needs to be there, and you're closest." My mother and sister had been spending the week in Florida. My brother, Steven, who, like my sister, was an assistant U.S. attorney in New York, was in court.

I got off the phone, went to the street, and caught a taxi. Until that day, nothing very dramatic had happened in my life. It was my first emergency, and I had no intention of blowing it. I went straight to the airport and used my new credit card to buy a ticket I could not afford, then sat at the gate reading the opening pages of *The Moviegoer* by Walker Percy.

This morning I got a note from my aunt asking me to come for lunch. I know what this means. Since I go there every Sunday for dinner and today is Wednesday, it can mean only one thing: she wants to have one of her serious talks. It will be extremely grave, either a piece of bad news about her stepdaughter Kate or else a serious talk about me, about the future and what I ought to do. It is enough to scare the wits out of anyone, yet I confess I do not find the prospect altogether unpleasant.

I was surprised by my calm. My heart did not race; my mind did not reel. I felt nothing. *Why aren't I panicking?* I asked myself. *Do I love my father? Do I love anyone? Am I some kind of psychopath?*

I expected to find Herbie alone in a hospital room, fighting for his life, but he was surrounded by people when I got there, doctors and nurses who were laughing as Herbie and Larry, who'd beat me to the hospital, were telling the Moppo story. Herbie was connected to machines, and was wearing one of those smocks, but he had lost all that weight and was tan and looked better than he had in years. "Good, I'm glad you're here," he said, when I came in. "Tell these people, would you, that there really is a Who Ha and that there really is an Inky. They don't believe us."

Larry, having experienced multiple heart attacks and multiple surgeries before the age of fifty—he'd even written a book called *"Mr. King, You're Having a Heart Attack"*—was what Grandma Esther would call "a real expert." Sitting on the edge of the bed after the staff had cleared out, he told Herbie exactly what to expect. "Your aortic valve is failing, but you'll soon have a new one. Maybe a pig valve, maybe titanium, though if it's pig you're probably going to want to get clearance from a rabbi, right? They'll start by putting you so deeply under anesthesia it'll be like you're gone. Then they'll cut you open, crack your rib cage, pop it like the hood of a car. They'll stop your heart by covering it in ice and put you on a heart-lung machine. It'll keep the blood flowing, the oxygen moving. The surgeon will take your heart out of your chest. Amazing, right? That guy who was just in here will be holding your heart in his hand! He'll cut out the old valve and replace it with a new one, put your heart back in your chest, then get it restarted with a jolt of electricity, just like when you jump the Caddy."

Herbie's mood changed as Larry spoke, though Larry didn't seem to notice. By the time my mother and sister arrived, he was gloomy and fighting with the doctors. It was Tuesday. They wanted to operate Thursday morning; it would take that long to assemble the best team. But Herbie had decided he did not want to be operated on in D.C. at all, but would instead fly to LaGuardia and get a cab to Cornell hospital, where my cousin David worked, because whatever is being done is being done better in New York.

The GW cardiologist at first refused to sign a release, then seemed to change his mind, saying, "Okay. I'll sign it and even come with you to the airport."

"Why?"

"Because someone will have to sign the death certificate."

Ellen sobbed when the doctor said this, saying, "Oh, Herbie, you're such a schmuck."

Herbie fell back and sighed.

"Fine," he said, staring at the wall. "Thursday morning."

I left to check in at a hotel and take a shower. When I got back at 10:00 p.m., Herbie's room was empty, his stuff was gone, and the bed was made. I was confused. Was I in the wrong room? Just then, Sharon came in holding a shredded T-shirt.

"What's that?"

She stared at the shirt for a time, then said, "It's Dad's," then burst into tears.

His valve had failed shortly after I left. He'd been rushed into emergency surgery.

"What about assembling the best team?" I asked.

"He was going to die," said Sharon.

They'd taken him at 9:00 p.m. They were still operating when the sun came up in the morning. At 5:00 a.m., my sister and brother took my mom down to the cafeteria. I was alone when the nurse came in.

She said, "The surgeons can't get your father off the heart-lung machine."

"What does that mean?"

"They can't get his heart beating."

The door opened. It was my brother, sister, and mother. My sister looked at me and knew something was wrong. But before I could say anything, a second nurse stuck her head in and shouted, "It's okay. He's off the machine. He's out of surgery."

They wheeled him past on the way to the ICU. He looked lifeless, inanimate, cold, and blue. My weird detachment evaporated in an instant. I fell through the floor and back into reality. I nearly burned on reentry. Bile rose in my throat. I reeled, turned, ran—down the hall, down the stairs, through the lobby, and into the dirty light of morning, where I found a hedge and puked into it.

No. 42

I GOT A FEW HOURS OF SLEEP AT THE HOTEL, THEN RE-turned. It was early afternoon, though it's always midnight in the cardiac ward. We were allowed to visit Herbie in twos. My mother and sister went first. I could see them through the windows of the heavy ICU doors. Ellen was bent over, touching Herbie as she spoke. Sharon had one hand on Ellen and another on the railing of the bed. They came out holding each other, crying.

Steven and I went in. Herbie was in a super-complicated hospital bed. There were wires and monitors. The machines had him. He looked the same as he had that morning: all death, no life; all body, no soul. He opened his eyes and gazed at us in confusion. He did not know who we were. He tried to talk, but was intubated. He'd repeatedly tried to pull out the tube, which is why his wrists had been tied to the bed.

"He doesn't know what's good for him," a nurse explained.

Tall with long gray hair, this nurse became the focus of Herbie's anger.

A sheet was thrown over his body, but it shifted and we could see the jagged scar. They'd given him a titanium valve and bypassed four of his arteries. Looking at him, I felt the way I'd felt the last time. Beds, walls, floor—it all began to spin. Steven grabbed my arm. I pulled away, turned, ran— past my sister and mother, through the hall, down the stairs, through the lobby, and back to the hedge.

Steven was waiting in the lobby when I returned.

We went into the coffee shop.

"You've got to control yourself," he said.

"How do *you* do it?"

"Did you see the big tube going down his throat?"

"Yes."

"I tell myself that Dad is Jacques Cousteau, and that the tube is connected to his oxygen tank, and that his eyes are wild because he's swimming around a beautiful reef."

Steven made swimming motions, then said, "Picture him that way, with bubbles coming up."

From then on, whenever the room started to spin, I'd look at Steven and he'd make the swimming motion and I'd be okay.

Despite the ventilator, Herbie found ways to communicate. Using just his eyes, he persuaded Ellen to pour a bucket of water over his head. As Ellen started to do this, the gray-haired nurse rushed over and scolded her. As she went away in a huff, Herbie, though his arms were still tied to the bed, gave the nurse the finger with both hands, the so-called double bird, which is when I knew he'd recover.

He was taken off the ventilator and moved to a regular room. Once he was settled, Ellen went to the Watergate gym to retrieve the clothes and wallet he'd left behind. She was in a good mood when she left and in a fury when she got back.

The gym manager told her he was the one who'd called the ambulance. Ellen asked where Herbie passed out. The manager said a trainer found him "slumped on the StairMaster."

"You promised," she screamed. "I told you, and you promised."

Herbie swore he'd never used the StairMaster.

"Then why'd they find you there?"

Herbie was quiet for a moment, thinking.

"I'm not sure," he said. "I was on the treadmill when I got dizzy. I pressed the emergency stop and got off. I must've stumbled up onto the StairMaster as I passed out."

He said that he'd fainted while running on the treadmill several times that summer and was often hurled across the room. If you'd been working out at the Watergate on one of those days, there was a good chance you would have seen the world's greatest negotiator in flight.

The week that followed surgery was tough. Herbie was an emotional whirligig, up and down, bright and bleak, warm and cold, sometimes elated to be alive, sometimes terrified not merely by how close he'd come but by how it made life seem arbitrary and meaningless. I could die now, or I could die in ten years. What's the difference?

I sat by his bed for hours, reading him the newspaper or watching TV.

"You have to be more careful," I said. "What would we do without you?"

I expected him to laugh when I said this or chuck me on the arm, but he wept instead. I'd never seen him cry like that. He said he could not stop thinking about how short he'd fallen from the goals he'd once set for himself. I scoffed at this, then told him what he had told his own father in the hospital: "You've done great."

"No, I haven't," he said. "All I've ever done is what I think my father would have done."

But maybe that's all anyone has ever done.

No. 43

HERBIE WAS PRESCRIBED SLEEPING PILLS THE NIGHT BEfore his release: Halcion, a Benzoid later taken off the market because it can cause temporary psychosis. Halcion is what made Philip Roth and George H. W. Bush go temporarily nuts. Such a narcotic does not change a person's character, but brings out what's normally been hidden, sublimated. It reveals a person's true nature. President Bush made a mockery of himself on Halcion, falling and vomiting into the lap of the Japanese prime minister. Philip Roth was overcome by paranoia on Halcion, a mental state depicted in his novel *Operation Shylock*.

Herbie took his Halcion at 10:00 p.m., was asleep by 11:00 p.m., and was more fully awake than he'd ever been at 3:00 a.m. He got out of bed and walked through the hospital, and as he walked those endless Kubrickian halls, he was tormented by the unfairness of the world. How is it right, he asked himself, holding his smock closed and creeping so as not to arouse attention, that some patients have many flowers, while others have none? He spent the rest of that long night correcting the injustice, stealing daffodils and tulips from the flower-rich and leaving them at the bedsides of the flower-poor. Exhausted when he got under the covers at dawn, he slept the sleep of the righteous, believing that he'd finally achieved the important work of his life.

No. 44

HIS GLOOM RETURNED AS SOON AS THE NOVELTY OF BEING back home faded. It fell on him like a cloud. Food lost its flavor, as did everything. The color drained from life, and what remained was a black-and-white simulation. It was as if he'd died on the table and woken in a different world altogether.

Depression is not uncommon in the aftermath of heart surgery. No one knows exactly why. Some believe it's the lingering effect of the anesthesia, traces of which can remain in a person's system for months. Some believe that the trauma of the surgery changes the chemical balance in the brain, that it can take up to a year to restore stasis. Some believe it's simply the patient's dawning realization of the human predicament revealed by the near-death encounter. Everyone knows they're going to die, but a person who's been through that knows it in a different way. In other words, there is knowing, and then there is *knowing*; there is understanding, and then there is accepting; it's the difference between the what and the how.

Being a productive person means believing you might live forever, that there is a point to all this work and suffering, that some of the achievements might survive, but for those who have leaned over and looked down, such belief becomes exceedingly difficult. To continue on as before, they have to forget what they've learned, which seems to take about a year.

Herbie returned to the road, but without joy. He was

going through the motions. Whereas he'd always seemed to move effortlessly through the world, you could now see him counting steps, making himself do it because there was nothing else to be done. Then, one day, he seemed better, lighter, happier. And the next day, he seemed happier still. About fifteen months after he'd collapsed, he took me for lunch at Duke Zeibert's in Washington, D.C. Though he'd been told to avoid red meat and fat, he ordered a filet with a side of creamed spinach.

Me: "Are you crazy? That stuff will kill you."

Him: "You've seen what I've been through. If that didn't kill me, nothing will."

No. 45

HERBIE HAD SOON REVERTED IN EVERY ARENA OF LIFE: diet, work, confrontation. He was back at full steam, giving hundreds of speeches a year, traveling all night to partake in negotiations. He'd given up cigars after he left the hospital, then, without explanation, began smoking again. When asked why, he'd say, "You're crazy. I never quit cigars." When we insisted, he said, "If I did quit like you say, I don't remember it, which is the same as if I didn't."

Then he did quit, only, once again, he didn't. I spotted him coming out of Nat Sherman's cigar shop at Forty-Second Street and Fifth Avenue in Manhattan, carrying a box of Montecristos that he swore was a gift for a friend but he couldn't remember which friend. He'd always been terrible at lying. He left evidence of secret cigar smoking everywhere. Ashes on his sweater, butts in his car. In Miami Beach, he listened to a radio show called *Smoke This!?* When saying goodbye to a guest or caller, the host of the show would wish that person "long ashes."

He dissembled even when caught red-handed. You'd come upon him at a coffee shop on Lincoln Road, a cigar smoldering on a ledge nearby.

You'd say, "I thought you quit."

He'd say, "I did quit."

You'd point to the cigar on the ledge and say, "Then what's that?"

He'd look at the cigar, do a double take, then say, "That's not mine."

Turning into Columbo, you'd say, "So, you're telling me a man walked by here, placed a half-smoked cigar on a ledge behind you, then walked away, and you didn't even notice?"

"Or woman."

"What?"

"It could have been a woman."

If seriously confronted—"You're going to kill yourself!! Do you want to die?"—he'd respond in the way of Aesop, with a fable: "My father's brother was named Itzhik. He was my favorite uncle. And Itzhik was sick all the time. Diabetes, heart disease, cholesterol. He was like the Danny Kaye sandwich at the Carnegie Deli, an old man with everything. Then he got throat cancer! Poor guy. They took out his voice box. He had to hold this metal device to his throat when he wanted to talk. It made him sound like an electric razor. We went to see him after the surgery. He was sitting up in bed when we got there, eating a corned beef sandwich. My father's other brother, Nathan, snuck it past the nurses. Itzhik was on a strict diet. My father was furious and yelled at both brothers. Itzhik, who'd been enjoying this sandwich, put the metal device to his throat and said, 'If you can't have a good corned beef, then what's the point of living?'"

No. 46

MEANWHILE.

Grandpa Ben, looking to secure his legacy, had become a philanthropist in his old age, focusing most of his attention on Maimonides, a midsize hospital in Borough Park, Brooklyn. He gave millions to Maimonides, and even served as president. He was determined to turn the hospital into a world-class heart center. He financed a new building and named it for Abraham Gellman, Betty's brother who'd been killed in the Philippines during World War II. There is a bust of Uncle Abe in the lobby, along with his Purple Heart, Silver Star, and citation signed by President Truman. There's an Eisenstadt building, too, with a portrait of Ben the patriarch in the front office.

When a rich man gives millions to a conveniently located hospital, it's partly to help the community and partly so the doctors will save him when the Malamoufitz knocks. That's what makes Ben's story such a black comedy. In the fall of 1996, he began experiencing the same sorts of symptoms that had troubled Herbie. He went directly to Maimonides, where he was diagnosed with valve failure and scheduled for replacement surgery. In preparation, he was given a megadose of penicillin, which triggered an allergic reaction that nearly killed him. He was released after a week in intensive care, told he was now too weak and old to survive surgery, and sent home. Restless in Midwood, he began doctor shopping, looking for a second, third, fourth opinion, for anyone who would agree to replace his valve. "I'd rather die on the table," he said, "than sit in that house waiting."

After having been turned down by a dozen specialists, Ben called Ellen. Herbie's nephew David, the cardiologist, agreed to examine Ben, then agreed to assemble a team and perform the surgery. At this point, I feel like jumping into the computer, grabbing Ellen by the shoulders, and screaming, "Why? What good can come of it? If he lives, they'll never forgive you for being the person he turned to. And if he dies, they'll say you killed him."

The operation was performed at New York Hospital on York Avenue in Manhattan when Ben was eighty-nine years old. It went perfectly. Ben was back at home three days after surgery. He joked and told stories when we visited him, behaving unlike the man I had known my entire life. He hugged me and said he was sorry—he did not say for what—then hugged me again. Ellen basked in the glow, for once at ease in her childhood home. Betty was affectionate. Gladys said nothing. It was just a moment, but it was a good moment.

Ben went back to the hospital for a checkup a week later. What started as a routine exam turned into a disaster when the doctors discovered an infection in his chest. In most cases, the patient would've been treated with antibiotics. Ben's allergic reaction at Maimonides ruled this out. They reopened his incision and cleaned out the infection by hand, then left him in a medically induced coma in case they had to go back in. Betty stayed in the ICU for weeks, talking to Ben, calling him home. She'd say, "He's Odysseus. He's making his way back to me."

Ben never regained consciousness. When he died in April 1996, *The New York Times* headlined the obituary "Benjamin Eisenstadt, 89, a Sweetener of Lives."

Betty got into bed in Midwood after the funeral and basically stayed there the rest of her life. Neither Prozac nor lithium could touch her. Her bed was moved downstairs to be closer to Gladys. Meant to salve her loneliness, this only made things worse. According to documents filed after Betty's death, Gladys abused Betty mentally and physically in those months, withheld medication and food, threw dishes, and even hit her. That's when Gladys persuaded or forced Betty to change her will, disinheriting Ellen and her family, changing the crucial clause to read, "to Ellen and her issue I leave nothing."

The reason?

According to Aunt Gladys, it was because "Your mother killed Ben."

Herbie wanted to contest the will, as did my brother. They hired attorneys. The process began. Steven, who led the legal team, actually deposed Aunt Gladys in her room. It's a Jungian fantasy. Neither my sister nor I was told about this. It was kept from us out of fear that, being weak and sentimental, we would argue against going forward. And, when the secret slipped out, we did. We begged and then commanded Herbie to drop the lawsuit. We worried that the experience would extend the awful moment of disinheritance indefinitely, destroying our mother. You never find what you really need in court, anyway; no matter the outcome, the trial becomes the punishment.

No. 47

GLADYS SAT IN THE FRONT ROW AT BETTY'S FUNERAL. IT was her first trip out of the house in years. She had to see that her mother had in fact been buried, had to know, with the evidence of her own eyes, that the all-powerful little woman was truly dead.

Gladys walked with two canes. She was shrunken, but her curly black hair still had the old spring. Her cheeks were as red as candied apples. When I went over and held out my hand, she looked at it and me with hatred, then said, "I have no idea who you are."

She had come to show Ellen and her issue that she, Gladys, had been the winner. She'd gotten the money, and the house, and the furniture, and the jewelry, all of which she would in turn leave to her friend Sherry, Sherry's son, and a cat possibly named Toots.

When I explained the lawsuit to Uncle Marvin, saying, "My mother wanted acceptance and love," he said, "Yeah, well, that's not what you ask for in court; in court you ask for money." He was right about that, but he was wrong, too, because in this world, where symbols stand for reality, the most powerful symbol is money.

Herbie understood this in a way the rest of us, having been raised in relative comfort, never did. "Success in life is about creating options and keeping those options open and available as long as possible, and money does that," he explained. "What's more, it's never really about the money, not even when it came to my lawsuit or Betty's will. That is to say, it's not about the money. It's about the *money*."

No. 48

THERE IS A HOLE IN THIS BOOK. SOMETHING IS MISSING. I've noticed it every time I've reread these pages. It's my mother, Ellen Marilyn Eisenstadt, her hopes, dreams, and disappointments. She was the happiest and unhappiest person I've ever known.

When I close my eyes, I see her life all at once, at every age, in every way she could be—as she was in her childhood in Brooklyn, as she was at the soda fountain and in Midwood High School, as she was at the NYU cafeteria where she met Herbie, who'd made up a story to talk to her, as she was as a daughter, sister, and young wife, mother and grandmother. She is young in my memory and she is old, too, arguing with airport security who wants her to skip the normal procedures because of her age.

"Just how old do you think I am?"

She's dressed in the flower-covered shifts of the 1970s, the pantsuits of the 1980s, and the skirts of the 1990s and beyond, a blushing bride, a protective mother, an infuriated daughter, a wounded wife, and a doting grandma, a woman of handbags and perfumes and gifts, drunk and happy from a single glass of wine, a woman who, having quit smoking years before, still says, "I can feel my lungs getting pinker every day." Which I suppose is my way of saying it's not my mom as she was at a particular moment I remember, but her essence, the immortal quality that outlives each change in body, circumstance, and fashion, that survives every infirmity and is still and always alive to be talked to and comforted and communed with. Despite her great emotional tides, the ebb and flood, she was essentially a happy person with a philosophy so simple it was religious.

She did not want parties, did not want wealth or fame. She just wanted to be left in peace to enjoy her family. She wanted to stay at the hotel and order from room service. She wanted to take a hot shower—with good pressure—have a glass of wine, and watch the tribute to Broadway on PBS. She wanted to spend the evening alone with her husband. This made her happy even when she was frustrated with his quests, even when he refused to settle the lawsuit, even when she was fighting with her parents and worried about money.

When they were clicking, Herbie and Ellen fell into a comedic patter. They were George Burns and Gracie Allen, Bud Abbott and Lou Costello. She believed in immortality, but did not believe in God. She played sick on major Jewish holidays. She'd call down as we waited in the front hall, dressed for synagogue, to say she had a stomachache or migraine and couldn't go.

Herbie would plead with her, saying, "Please, it's just a few hours."

"Oh, Herbie," she'd say. "I don't believe in any of that."

I knew my mother didn't believe in God. She thought the whole thing was a fairy tale and that if you live on it's in the memories of those who love you, which was never good enough for me.

Herbie, as if to balance the example, expressed a strong and certain belief in God. When I pointed out contradictions in the Bible, he'd shrug me off, saying, "It's confusing because it's not our fate to know with certainty. It's mysterious and opaque for a reason. As the Book says, we can know what it is given to us to know, but the rest belongs to God. In other words, it's none of your business. Your business is to do what you're supposed to do and be good to other people."

To him, Judaism is as much about tradition as theology. Each generation, while living out its own life, was a kind of bridge, carrying the faith over the abyss, handing it off, as it had been handed over for hundreds of generations. No matter what else he did with his life he was determined to make that handoff, which is why he wanted my mother to go through the motions. Even if it doesn't seem important to you now, hang on to it, save it—leave the option open—because you never know how it'll look to you or what it might mean later. All it takes is one bad generation, one group of people who don't understand, for the signal to be lost, the thread snapped.

Ellen did not believe in that kind of tradition. To her, if it is not working, if it does not speak to you, it should be exchanged for something that does. When Herbie spoke of ancestors and descendants, she shook her head. She believed no one, no matter what they said, could truly care about more than five generations. "Your grandparents and parents, siblings, children, and grandchildren—beyond that, life is a path that emerges from darkness and returns to darkness."

Family is what made her happy, here and now, time in a bottle. She needed to love and be loved. She was like a hot-house flower, an orchid that requires a lot of attention. If you missed a day, she'd suffer. She was terrified of abandonment. But given proper care, she bloomed.

I made a list of things she liked and things she didn't like.

First the dislikes: the sound of children fighting; the way her mother talked on the phone; driving in the snow; driving at night; Larry King and his many wives; the raccoons in the attic; our dog Lazlo; baths, "because, in a bath, you're basically sitting in your own filth."

Now the likes: chocolate egg creams made with Fox's U-Bet syrup; musicals; Hitchcock movies; Charles Aznavour; Rome and Paris; jewelry; Herbie; four-star hotels; room service; wine in the afternoon; lemon vodka; her children.

Being a grandmother was best of all. It was all frosting and no cake—no getting up at 2:00 a.m., no punishing, withholding, driving to hockey, or preparing for the future. She loved J. D. Salinger and seemed to share his view about adulthood: that it crushes the wonder in us and sublimates natural joy and curiosity into something complicated and dark. Children are pure goodness and all love, and their presence reminds you that in the end only one thing matters.

She was a young grandmother, just fifty-three when my sister Sharon's first child was born. My brother and his wife, Lisa, soon followed. Ellen had seven grandchildren before she turned sixty-five. It changed her. She relaxed, filled out, began wearing blowsy clothes and flat shoes. She spent entire afternoons at FAO Schwarz.

This is where Herbie and Ellen parted for a time. He loved his grandkids, but did not like *being* a grandparent. Not at first, anyway. He did not want to be called Grandpa, only Herbie.

Or the nickname he fashioned for his new role, Mr. Strong Man. Sharon's and Steven's children would speak of visits from "Grandma Ellen and Herbie."

Becoming a grandparent seemed to shock and upset him. Though still in his fifties when his first grandchild was born, it registered as a portent of mortality. It was the grim reaper waiting with his coat at the door. It was a turn of the wheel. It was the change you feel when the sun passes its zenith.

He began skipping events, taking a last-minute powder. He went to the West Coast just to hang out with Larry and the Brooklyn boys.

He seemed edgy when he was with us, even a little angry.

"What's wrong with you?" I asked after dinner one night in D.C.

"What are you talking about?"

"You've been mean lately," I said.

"You're crazy."

"I'll tell you what's wrong with him," said Steven. "He's realizing that he won't be around forever and that he's not going to reach a lot of the goals he set for himself and that he's much closer to the end than to the beginning."

Steven was speaking as if analyzing a character in a story. I think he started out joking but the logic carried him away. He'd meant to be funny but wound up cutting too close to the bone.

"Is that true?" I asked my father.

"It's bullshit," said Herbie, more to himself than to us.

This is the context for what followed, the part of Herbie's life that remains a puzzle for me. It violated the rules he'd set for us over the years.

No. **49**

I MET HER BEFORE MY FATHER. IT WAS ON A TRIP TO LOS Angeles in the 1990s. She was ten years older than me, around forty, a short-haired brunette who worked in the movie business. She was dating my father's friend Sid, a part of the Brooklyn contingent that went west after high school. The age difference struck me as odd. Sid was old enough to be her father. I met her, then forgot her. Let's say her name was Penny. She was like one of those characters that take center stage at the end of a play, though they've been lurking in the background from the start.

Larry had married his ninth wife, Shawn, then, at her insistence, moved his CNN show to Los Angeles. Herbie began going out there to see Larry. He invited my mother, but she refused to go. Penny, who broke up with Sid, pulled Herbie aside during one of those visits. She said she knew about his work as a negotiator and needed help. She said she was being pushed out of her job and didn't know where to turn. That's really why it started: because he could never refuse a person being shafted by the machine.

At some point early in the twenty-first century, the relationship became physical. I don't know the details, and don't want to know. As far as I'm aware, Herbie, until then, had been with only one woman, my mother. For all his travels, he was, in some ways, inexperienced, naive. Maybe it was becoming a grandparent that did it. Maybe he wanted to know more of life before it was too late.

If there were good times, they did not last long. Within a

few months, Penny was pressuring Herbie. She wanted money, gifts, to be taken on vacation. When Herbie refused, she threatened to tell Ellen and the children everything. After he'd depleted his savings to placate her, she called my mother and told anyway.

How did we find out?

At Ellen's insistence, Herbie called each of his children and confessed what he'd done. He started by saying, "This is your father. I love you. I've made a terrible mistake."

Ellen made him do this not by way of punishment, or not entirely, but out of fear that this woman in Los Angeles would call each of us to tell on my father, as she had threatened and as she in fact did. That call from Penny wasn't the absolute worst call I've ever received.

What had Herbie been thinking?

What did he believe would happen after he'd run out of money and fixes? Instead of answering this question, I will share one of his favorite jokes, a joke that, as far as he is concerned, expresses an ancient philosophy made necessary by the vicissitudes of Jewish history: "The czar of Russia summoned the Minsk rabbi to the Kremlin, where he handed him a cage with a parrot and said, 'You have one year to teach this parrot to speak Latin.' The rabbi, accepting the challenge, returned home, where his wife, hearing the story, became hysterical. 'But you don't even know Latin,' she said. 'What are you going to do?'

"'A year is a very long time,' said the rabbi. 'A lot can happen in a year. First of all, the czar could die. Second, I could die. Or third, the parrot could die.'"

No. **50**

THE ENSUING WEEKS STAND AS A DISTINCT EPOCH, LIKE the Little Ice Age or the age of disco, consisting of my mother crying, my father apologizing and repenting and calling himself a schmuck.

I was disappointed by Herbie, but sympathetic, too. His brush with death, his fear of oblivion, the darkness ahead, his desire to live, his hunger for more life, which, to him, must have meant novelty, new experience, even danger, had pushed him to folly. The fact that he'd botched it so badly tells me he'd never done this kind of thing before; he was so awful at it. The subterfuge, the juggling, the phone calls and excuses—it blew up in his face almost as soon as he'd opened the package.

I was angry at myself, too. I should have known what was going on, and at a subliminal level maybe I did. I knew Herbie had been going to L.A. for no good reason. In other words, it was right in front of me, but I decided not to notice.

Worst of all, I'd actually had dinner with Herbie and Penny in L.A., where I'd gone for work, making me complicit. We went to Matsuhisa, the sushi restaurant in Beverly Hills where my friend Mark was maître d'. I was supposed to meet my father alone, but he showed up with Penny. He said he had bumped into her in the lobby of his hotel and, on a whim, had invited her along. They sat on one side of the table. I sat on the other. He seemed anxious to eat his meal, pay the check, and leave. It was so strange. Mark called me a few days later and asked if my father was dating the woman he'd brought to dinner. After I'd cursed out Mark for merely suggesting such a thing, he said, "In that case, do you mind if I ask her out?"

If I had any doubts, they were dispelled that fall, when we spent Thanksgiving weekend at my sister's house. I was working on a draft of my book *Lake Effect*, which was about my childhood on Chicago's North Shore. I'd given Herbie the manuscript a few weeks earlier, as I'd done with all my writing. This gets into Herbie's role as my shadow editor, which goes back to grade school. Sometimes he revised my papers. Sometimes he rewrote them, which explains the frequent mention of Bensonhurst and the Brooklyn Dodgers in my schoolwork.

There was good and bad in this.

Here's (some of) the good:

He always supported me, even after he'd stopped rewriting me. When my brother laughed at my dream of being published in *The New Yorker*, Herbie scolded him, saying, "What's funny? Richard's stuff is good enough for that magazine right now." Later, if he liked a story of mine that had been rejected, he'd say, "Forget it. It's a good story. Believe me: I know better than that editor. I've read more and lived more and I'm telling you it's good." When my first book was published, he did more than the publisher to sell it. He made clandestine trips to all the big bookstores, requested and extolled my book in a booming voice, bought three copies, then, when he thought no one was looking, moved the rest to the front of the display. He drummed up crowds for my events. He seeded the room with shills, Warriors like Inky and Who Ha, who raised their hands as soon as I'd finished talking, then asked questions written by Herbie, such as "How is it someone so young has written such a brilliant book?" Or: "Can you explain why I couldn't put this book down?"

Here's (some of) the bad:

In trying to help, he usually took control, pushing me out of my own process. He was like the friendly mobster who, after helping fix your problem, decides to stick around. He'd stand up at events and start explicating, delivering stem-winding testimony as if we were strangers, though most of the people in the audience knew exactly who he was—his picture was in the book! He'd pull me aside after each reading to share his "thoughts," which could be brutal. After soften-ing me with a few compliments, he'd criticize my voice, pro-nunciation, choices, and demeanor. "You read too goddamn fast. And need a shave! And a better shirt!" He gave me notes on the early drafts of my work; most of his suggestions were meant to either clarify, soften the hard edges—"because why piss people off? These are your readers"—or clean up the language.

"Who taught you to use these disgusting words?"

"You did?"

"Well, if I did, I didn't mean to."

But the notes he gave on *Lake Effect* were different.

While sitting at my sister's dining room table, he went through the manuscript. It was dog-eared, diner stained, rid-dled with paper clips and rubber bands, as well as two distinct kinds of handwriting—one familiar, one strange. He sug-gested the sorts of additions and changes you hear nowhere but in pitch sessions and the writing rooms of the movie in-dustry. He spoke of plot points and conflicts and takeaways. He spoke of backstories and B stories and reveals. He said,

"Maybe it turns out Jamie is gay. Or maybe you are gay. Or maybe you're both gay. Maybe you've just come back from the army. Maybe, though you don't know it until the third act, you and Jamie have the same father."

In other words, I chose not to know what I knew. Herbie says, "Believing is seeing." If true, then the opposite must also be true: "Not believing is not seeing."

There was tremendous fallout from the affair. Abandonment had always been Ellen's primal fear—being cast aside, left behind, forgotten. Herbie's infidelity was Ellen's biggest fear realized. There was some talk of divorce, but none of us took it seriously. Herbie and Ellen had been married for more than forty years. They'd grown together like old trees, roots entangled, leaves forming a single awesome canopy. Ellen instead chose to erase all evidence of the affair from her life and her mind.

Because Penny had possibly visited these places, the apartments in Washington, D.C., and Miami Beach were sold. Before a month was out, Herbie and Ellen had moved from South Beach to a ranch house beside a golf course in a country club in Delray Beach, the exact sort of nondescript place my father hated. Asked the average age of residents at the Boca Delray, he'd say, "Comatose." They closed the deal after a single quick walk-through—bought it fast, everything included, even furniture, even sheets, and even tchotchkes. "I've always wanted tchotchkes," said Ellen when she showed me the house. When I pointed out that these were not her tchotchkes, she said, "Oh, Richard, tchotchkes are tchotchkes."

I sometimes wondered if Herbie strayed less to satisfy himself than to release his children. His example was so strong it could be suffocating. It was impossible to live up to. Maybe he did what he did to set us free. Of course, I know that this is not what he intended. The man simply faltered. He simply gave in to restlessness. He simply behaved like a human being. It was a perfect example of the old man teaching by counterexample, of his kids taking away a lesson but not the lesson he had intended. There was the *what* (Herbie instructing his children not to "sacrifice a mature design to gratify a momentary passion") and the *how* (Herbie, Penny, and me splitting a dragon roll at Matsuhisa). The *what* was the ideal—the way a person should behave. The *how* was what life is like in the real world, where even our heroes falter.

Being in the new house—a place without associations— did not fix Ellen right away. That took years. But she did forgive him, and once she did, it was as if it never happened. And then came the great gift of her later years. One afternoon, after Betty and Ben and Gladys had all died, Ellen's brother Marvin called and cried on the phone and said he had been wrong and she had been right and everything they had told her was in her head was in fact true: she had been treated unfairly, frozen out of the family, given over to placate Gladys, who was angry in a way none of the others could face or understand. "We were scared of her, and the way we dealt with it was awful and wrong," he said.

When Herbie heard this, he said, "He must be seeing

a new therapist. Let's see if he ponies up the do-re-mi." He did. But this was better than money. Everyone in this world believes they got a raw deal, were mistreated, could have made much more of themselves if they'd gotten a fair shake. But almost no one gets what Ellen got—a call telling them they are not crazy but had in fact been right all along. With that, the cloud that had followed my mother since childhood lifted.

No. 51

ONCE UPON A TIME, THERE WAS A YOUNG COUPLE. THEY were married, had children, lived their lives. They started out in the front row of family pictures. Then moved to the middle, where they posed behind their children. Then, before they had time to note the change, were pushed into the last row, the place reserved for matriarchs and patriarchs. A step back and they'd tumble out of the frame altogether.

After living in Brooklyn, Long Island, New Jersey, Libertyville, Glencoe, Washington, and Miami Beach—a new house or apartment in each town, a new street with new friends and new habits—they found themselves in this palm-fringed bungalow astride the third fairway of the Boca Delray Golf and Country Club. There was a player piano in the living room, a bathroom walled with mirrors—you could see parts of your body you'd never even imagined—a screened-in pool where shanked tee shots drummed down like hail.

Several of the old Warriors—excluding Larry and the West Coast contingent—were vegetating in nearby communities with opulent names. The Shangri Shalom. The Heavenly Heathen. Herbie and Ellen began gathering with these aging Brooklynites in the afternoon in this or that house or condo. They had known each other since grade school. They had been fourteen when Japan surrendered. They had lived through it all. The Cold War. Nuclear terror. Nixon and Clinton. The collapse of the Berlin Wall. Being a little old for rock and roll, they had stayed with the classics—Sinatra, Nat King Cole. When I asked Herbie how he'd missed the Beatles—he was thirty when they appeared on *Ed Sullivan*—he said, "I was too busy working." They had seen America at its apex, had seen the boom and what appears to be the decline.

There were usually five or six old Warriors at these get-togethers, some of whom I'd known all my life, some of whom I'd known only from stories. Bernie Horowitz, Who Ha, who was still married to Honey and still described himself as a "manufacturer's representative"; Inky Kaplan, who'd been only the second white student to attend the Howard University College of Dentistry; Arnie Perlmutter, who was short with supernaturally long arms, "which," said Herbie, "is what made him such a devastating softball pitcher"; Brazie Abbate, who'd never fully recovered from the Moppo thing, was a brain surgeon with practices in Asheville, North Carolina, and Beijing, China; Mal Afchin, who'd been a great athlete in his day—he played Division 1 college basketball—and who worked for IBM; Bucko had been an army MP in Korea, a runner for the mob, a grifter, a stock car racer, a legend on the dirt ovals of the Southeast, then a real estate broker in Florida. It seemed funny, the fact that no matter what these men had done or achieved in their lives, they ended up back together, in the same place, drinking the same wine in the same marble-floored rooms. (Nothing poses a greater threat to the elderly than wet marble.) One of the wives had T-shirts made up for the men ("Aging Warrior") and for the women ("Aging Warriors Ladies Auxiliary").

I loved going to their events, listening to the small talk and stories. Once, when Arnie was trying to remember where he'd played YMCA basketball, he turned to Mal and said, "Hey, Mal. Do you remember that Turkish place where we had dinner a few years ago in the city? You got a stomachache and had to leave early. Do you remember the address?"

"I remember," said Mal. "It was on Tenth Street and Second Avenue. Only it wasn't a stomachache I had, you schmuck! It was a heart attack! Remember the large white vehicle with flashing lights that took me away?"

Ellen loved these get-togethers, then didn't. "It's depressing," she told me. "Every time we go, they tell us someone else is dead."

The last time they gathered as a group was at Mal Afchen's funeral. The rabbi, who had not known any of the Warriors, eulogized Mal in the generic way of a clergyman working off someone else's notes. He said Mal had been a member of a gang called the Warriors, which had a clubroom in the basement of a house owned by Larry King.

Who Ha shouted when the rabbi said this: "Bullshit! That was my house. Larry had no fucking house. Larry lived in an apartment."

Herbie shushed Who Ha, who snapped at him, saying, "No, I won't shush. Larry got famous, so what? Does that mean everything that happened to me gets attributed to him?"

"Hey, Bernie, who gives a fuck about your house?" said Herbie. "Let's remember why we're here. See that box up there? Our friend Mal is in that fucking box."

Larry's fame had long been a distraction. To most of the Warriors, it was exciting in the way Koufax's success had been. It connected them to the upper world. It put the landscape of their childhood on the map. Who Ha hated it. Every mention of Larry—"Did you grow up with Larry King?" "Did you know Larry King before he was famous?"—felt like Zeke the Creek giving him the high hat. When Herbie and Larry arrived at a reunion in a hired car, Who Ha went wild. "What? You think you're special because you got a limo? I can get a limo here in ten minutes. Let me make a call and I'll have a limo and then I'll be a big shot too." Who Ha made the call. When the Warriors stumbled out at midnight, Who Ha's car was waiting by the curb. "Now I'm a big shot too!" he said.

No. 52

HERBIE FINALLY COMPLETED HIS SEQUEL TO *YOU CAN Negotiate Anything*. It was called *Negotiate This! By Caring, but Not T-H-A-T Much*. He went on tour for the book, did all the shows, including that of Dr. Phil, who wired a few average shoppers so Herbie, watching on a screen in an unmarked van, could talk them through deals, coaching them to say things like "You know what, I don't need it after all." Or: "Can I see a floor model?" Or: "What kind of ties will you be throwing in with this?" According to the website, "Dr. Phil sent Claire jewelry shopping with a hidden camera. Meanwhile Herbie watched from a van outside. When the saleswoman put a bracelet—costing $1,050—around Claire's wrist, Claire commented how lovely it is. 'Look at that,' said Herbie. The sales woman 'wants Claire to fall in love with this bracelet. This should not be an emotional purchase.'"

Herbie, who'd been famous in his forties, became something of a cult figure in his later years, name-checked in books and by stand-up comedians and on TV shows. He was a leitmotif in the first season of Mike Judge's *Silicon Valley*. Whenever a character closed a deal, another would say, "You're our own Herb Cohen!"

Asked by *Mediaite* to bring his analytical skills to pop culture, he delivered a weekly commentary on the needs, motivations, and tactics of *The Real Housewives of New York City*, a show he watched with an intensity he'd once reserved for televangelists. "In my time—remember, I'm an old guy—we had Mickey Rooney and Judy Garland putting on shows in a barn where there was dancing and singing," he explained. "This show is this generation's Mickey and Judy."

"Luann arrives to meet Jill in a rickshaw pulled by a bike and the rider of that bike is a black guy, so now," Herbie said after one scene, "they've integrated the show."

"If you're in a conversation and someone should walk over and publicly call you a slut and a whore," he said, after another, "keep your composure and calmly reply, 'That's a lovely dress.'"

As Sharon's and Steven's kids progressed through high school, he became fixated—obsessed—by the question of where they'd go to college. He compiled exhaustive lists, breaking hundreds of universities down according to reputation, cost, quality. When one of his grandchildren complained, he'd talk about life and how it's a race and how the track on which you run that race is divided into lanes and how the person in a good school starts on an inside lane while a person in a less good school starts on an outside lane and so must work harder and run faster to reach the same place.

Calling in from the next room, Sharon would say, "Is he talking about the lanes?"

He'd dreamed of sending us to Yale, which he'd idealized ever since his snowy midnight ride through New Haven with Who Ha, Larry, and Sandy. When he realized it was not in the cards, he admonished me, saying, "If you'd done better, you could've gone to Yale."

"No," I said. "If *you'd* done better, I could have gone to Yale."

When his grandchildren likewise failed, he chose to live in fantasyland, telling an alumni coordinator from my high school—they were putting together a directory—that I had in fact gone to Yale.

"That's not what we have," she said. "We have his college as Tulane."

"Well, you have it wrong," he said.

"It clearly says Tulane University class of 1990."

"If you're so certain," asked Herbie, "then why are you calling?"

"Just to confirm."

"Fine. Consider it confirmed. He went to Yale."

No. 53

I NEVER WORRIED ABOUT ELLEN'S HEALTH. IN COMPARI-
son to Herbie, she seemed rock solid, bulletproof. She was
always thirty-five in my mind, blasting down the expressway
with Helen Reddy on the tape deck. Which is why I thought
nothing of it when Herbie called to say my mother had
checked into a hospital in Delray Beach with stomach pains.

My siblings and I devised a plan: they'd fly to Florida to
help my father; then, if my mother was still in the hospital on
Monday, I'd take their place.

At 2:00 p.m., Herbie called to say Ellen had been diagnosed with pancreatitis, which a doctor described as "painful
but not serious"; with antibiotics, she was expected to recover
quickly. He called back at 6:00 p.m. to say her condition had
worsened. Asked to rank her pain from one to ten, Ellen
said "ten"—"but that's not unusual," said the doctor. "She
should rebound in the next few hours." Herbie called again at
8:00 p.m. to say the doctor, confused by her failure to respond
to treatment, had sent her for more tests. At 10:00 p.m., Herbie called to say the diagnosis had been changed from pancreatitis to ischemia.

"What's that?" I asked.

"I don't know," he said. "Do a Google."

I looked it up when we got off the phone.

"My father got something wrong," I told my wife, Jessica.
"He says that she has ischemia, but according to this, if she
has ischemia, she's going to die."

My sister began calling with reports as soon as she arrived

in Florida. Her voice was calm on the phone, but there was a tone of disbelief.

At noon on the second day, she called and said, "You need to fly down here."

"When?"

"Now."

It was less hospital than jacked-up urgent care center, a glass building off Military Trail in Delray. My family was sitting around my mother's bed in the ICU—my father, my sister, my brother, and my father's sister, Renee. Steven was joking, but nothing seemed very funny. My mother, who'd been coherent a few hours before, had already begun to slip away. Her eyes were open but lost and searching.

We sat around the bed and talked over and about but not to my mother. Herbie was in the corner, sitting quietly. A doctor told us what was happening—she did indeed have ischemia; she was being attacked by her own immune system—but none of it registered with me. My wife later said that each time we spoke on the phone, my news was worse, but I didn't seem to realize it. I'd say, "The ischemia has brought on sepsis, but they're treating it, and she'll be home by the end of the week." I'd say, "She's going to need rehab, but they're treating it, and she'll be home by the end of the week." You prepare yourself for the big moment, then don't even notice when it arrives. I thought I was passing time while my mother was being treated. It was only later that I realized I was watching my mother die.

We went back to the house to get some sleep. It was the middle of the night. I don't know what time. The doctors were going to operate in the morning. They'd fix her. She'd be home by the end of the week.

The phone woke me. I looked at the clock: 2:47 a.m. It rang and rang but no one stirred. I wandered through the dark, looking for an extension. I picked it up and said hello. A nurse told me that my mother was coding, which I later learned means her heart had stopped. "They're working on her," said the nurse, "you should probably get back here."

The hospital door was locked. We banged and banged until a janitor let us in. A nurse was waiting. She said the doctors had been able to restart our mother's heart. She was going to be okay, I told myself, she'll be home by the end of the week.

The surgeon arrived at 6:00 a.m. He took us into the hall. He was Israeli. I don't remember his exact words, but they were something like "Your mother is going to die. We are going to operate so you won't feel like you left anything untried."

We waited in the lobby while they prepped her for surgery. We were sitting in chairs along a wall. The sun had risen, but it still felt like night. The electric door opened and a clown came in. This did not seem like an official hospital clown, the sort hired to entertain kids. This clown was dirty and smelled bad. She wore whiteface and a wig of loose red curls. She scanned the room, then fixed on me. I was holding an iPhone. She grinned and said, "It looks like someone's sad! Don't be sad!" Taking the phone from my hand, she yelled, "SELFIE!" leaned close, turned, and took a picture. After she'd left, my brother said, "Can you please send me a copy of that picture?"

"Why?"

"I want to look at it whenever I need to remember what life is like."

Sharon went to check on my mom, then rushed out to get us. My mother had gone back into cardiac arrest. She was coding. We stood by the bed as doctors and nurses shocked her with paddles. Each jolt sent her into the air. It went on and on. Then they stopped. A doctor looked at his watch and said, "Ten twenty a.m." Someone wrote that down. Someone else led us to the interfaith chapel, a room with nothing in it. We stood there for a while, staring at the walls. Another nurse came and took us back to say goodbye to our mother. They'd cleaned her up. We stood around, kissing her face, then went home and started making phone calls.

No. 54

I DON'T KNOW WHAT KILLED MY MOTHER. ONE MINUTE she was fine; the next minute she was gone. She failed so fast. Ischemia was the ultimate cause, but what caused the ischemia? It might have been bad luck, like rolling snake eyes. Or it might have been hereditary, something in her genes. I suspect it was something she swallowed, one of the pills she'd been prescribed by one of those shady Broward County doctors. Herbie later cursed himself for not paying closer attention to her habits. He wished he'd studied the labels and intervened. But the fact is, my parents enabled each other in that stucco house in Delray. She did not judge him and he did not judge her. One night, Ellen spotted a cockroach on the wall near the ceiling. What started as my father on a stepladder with a broom ended with both of them in the hospital and the cockroach still very much alive.

No. 55

THE FUNERAL WAS IN MANHATTAN. HERBIE WAS TOO UP-
set to speak. My brother, sister, and I took his place. We drove
together in one car to the cemetery in Valhalla, New York.
My mother had not been afraid to die. She often spoke of it
as a good thing, a state of nonbeing she craved. She believed
that life without death would be insufferable, that death is
what makes life valuable and gives it meaning. Once, when I
asked her what she thought happens when you die, she said,
"Whatever you want to happen, that's what will happen to
you."

No. 56

WE FIGURED HERBIE WOULD NOT SURVIVE A YEAR WITH-
out Ellen. Not only did he love her, but he relied on her; she
did everything. Ordered his meals, apportioned his pills,
booked his flights, bought his clothes. He did not even know
how to use an ATM. He did not even own a bank card or cell
phone. He had not paid a bill in fifty years. It was not grief
that would kill Herbie but lack of heat or water. Or he'd forget to take his blood thinner and have a stroke. Or he'd take
it, forget he'd taken in, take it again, bump into a chair, and
bleed to death. He bought a roast chicken in a seedy deli a
few weeks after my mother died, ate some of it, left the rest
on the counter, ate that a few days later, then was rushed to
the hospital with food poisoning. Here's the first thing he
said when I called: "I never would've eaten that chicken if
your mother was alive."

But we underestimated him. After a few months, he began to recover, even rally. He sold the Florida house and moved to Brooklyn. He was the same, but the borough had changed. He made new friends. He fell in with a social group, a clique, that, oddly, included Tony Danza. He'd advise Danza on the set list for his musical act, saying, "You want to bring 'em down in the middle, Tony, but leave 'em up at that end, which always means Cole Porter."

He was named to the planning committee for the Feast of San Gennaro, the only non-Italian to have the honor. ("At a certain age, Italians and Jews become indistinguishable," he explained.) He served as a judge of the big meatball-eating contest that ended the festival. ("My job is to make sure none of the winners vomit.") He began dating a woman he met in a bereavement group. When he told us about this relationship, he did it gingerly. If he diminished her, or so he seemed to think, we would not take it as an insult to our mother. "Her name is Roseanne. She's a little younger than me, but she will never replace your mother. Your mother was the most beautiful person I have ever known."

When I asked if I was too old to yell, "You're not my mother. You can't tell me what to do," at Roseanne, then bolt the dinner table, he dismissed me as "a wise guy."

Most amazingly, he continued to work, fielding calls, negotiating fees, booking gigs. He lectured around the country and world, but there was a new lilt to his voice, a new resonance to his routine. He spoke with the wisdom of the old-timer whose every aphorism—"money talks, but it doesn't tell the truth"; "the fish doesn't know it's in the water"—seems to possess a deeper meaning. Condé Nast hired him to teach its

international staff how to negotiate in Southeast Asia. He says he loves working in China because, in China, age is considered wisdom. He trained European execs how to operate in Russia, how to deal with what he still calls "the Soviet style." "Against a stubborn opponent," he says, "it's better to be stupid than smart."

People have died all around him, but he keeps going, retooling his shtick to meet the needs of a different generation, instructing the young in the Jedi art. He's not quite as fast as he used to be, but what's been lost in speed is made up for in perspective. His business strategy has deepened into philosophy. He's a Brooklyn Buddha preaching detachment: "Life is a game best played at a remove; the secret is to care, but not that much."

My brother persuaded him to reprise his screening and analysis of *12 Angry Men* for a group in Brooklyn Heights. It had been years, but according to Steven, who sent the picture on the preceding page, he was just as good as ever.

"How'd he end it?" I asked.

"You know how he ended it," said Steven.

He kept meeting people who said his books had been part of their lives. They felt as if he'd been with them when they bought their first car, closed their first deal, tried to reason with their kids.

No. 57

I WROTE A PROFILE OF LARRY KING FOR *ROLLING STONE* IN 1996. I spent a week with Larry at La Costa, the California health spa built with Teamster money by Jimmy Hoffa. Larry told me the story of his life, which is also my father's story. Larry was coming off yet another heart procedure—the man was held together by tape, bubble gum, staples, and glue—when we spoke. He said he believed in nothing beyond this life and planned to live forever. "And do me a favor," he added. "Let's say I end up in a hospital, and I'm filled with tubes, and there's no brain activity, the line is flat, and machines are keeping me alive, don't let them unplug me! Keep everything in the wall. And if you see a loose cord, plug that in, too."

And that's basically what happened. Larry spent the last few years of his life in and out of hospitals. Herbie went to visit him at Cedars-Sinai in L.A. in 2019. Larry, who'd had cancer and a stroke, was in intensive care. Herbie felt sick just looking at Larry and ended up in the hospital himself, in a bed down the hall. You know it's bad when you visit a friend and the doctors don't let you leave. My sister, brother, and I went out to retrieve our father—it was his gallbladder—and stopped in to see Larry. He looked terrible, skin and bones. He pointed a bony finger at me and said, "Writer."

That was the last time any of us saw Larry, including Herbie. A few weeks later, COVID broke, forcing everyone, especially octogenarians, to shelter in place. Larry died in January 2021. My father had not spoken to him on the phone in a few weeks—the longest they'd gone without talking since the 1970s.

This made my father, a man you might have picked to go early, one of only a handful of surviving Warriors. (Inky, the orthodontist, is still taking appointments.) A new kind of freedom has come with age. There are richer and more powerful people than Herbie, but no one outranks him. No one is above or beyond. He can say what he wants without feeling bad; he can do what he wants without asking permission or calculating the extended effects. Longevity, survival—these have been added to his list of accomplishments, how he's continued to participate in the world even as everything in it has changed.

When COVID-19 swept through New York in 2020, he accepted it with equanimity.

"You'll be fine," he said. "Your kids will be fine. I'm the one who will probably die, and, let's be honest, that's no tragedy."

The quarantine robbed us of time together, but spurred me to call him more often, to spitball, interrogate, and ask to hear all the old stories again.

Tired of skirting the big question, one day I finally just came out and asked it: "What's the meaning of life?"

"The meaning of life?" he said, laughing. "Don't you know? The meaning of life is that there is no meaning of life, none we can know. That's not your business anyway. Your business is to be a decent person, raise nice kids, and keep going as long as you can.

"The meaning of life," he said at last, "is more life."

ACKNOWLEDGMENTS

I am indebted to my wife, Jessica, for her close reading, re-reading, and cutting of the various drafts of this book. I would also like to thank the members of my family who lived it before me and are living it still: Sharon Levin, Steven Cohen, Herbert Cohen, and Ellen Eisenstadt Cohen, who is here even if the phone book and Facebook say she's not. I'd like to thank Jonathan Galassi, for telling me when my shoes are untied and having me run it again. And, as always, thanks to Francis Albert Sinatra.